Uncover Your Message

Written by a non-native English-speaking professional speaker with over 20 years of international consulting experience, this book lays out a step-by-step process to improve cross-cultural communication skills and achieve a strong global presence.

Every year, organizations lose money, time, and people due to poor or inefficient cross-cultural communication – and this can be as easily between departments or individuals within an organization as across oceans. To tackle this widespread problem, Natsuyo N. Lipschutz developed the 3-step process she calls the "3As" (Acknowledge, Analyze, Adapt), using a unique multilayered approach: cross-culture × logical thinking × storytelling. Using the 3As process, readers will improve their awareness of cultural differences and learn analytical and logical thinking skills to zero in on their own unique message, tell persuasive stories, and ultimately get their messages not only clearly heard but acted upon in a culturally diverse global business environment.

Filled with lessons and real-life stories from global companies and executives who benefited from Natsuyo's guidance, this book will appeal to any business leader who needs to communicate with a diverse range of stakeholders, whether in a different country or a different team, to persuade and succeed.

Natsuyo N. Lipschutz, CSP®, MBA, Japanese native and New Yorker at heart, Natsuyo traveled 7,000 miles to start her cross-cultural business career in the United States. A keynote speaker, cross-cultural communication strategist, TEDx speaker, cancer survivor, and ballroom Latin dancer, Natsuyo shares colorful stories behind her cross-cultural communication strategies. Today, she is the founder and managing principal of ASPIRE Intelligence and Breakthrough Speaking, helping global organizations elevate cultural inclusion and have their leaders communicate effectively beyond differences.

Uncover Your Message

The 3-Step Process for Presenting
Your Ideas Effectively and Persuasively,
Globally and Locally

Natsuyo N. Lipschutz

Routledge
Taylor & Francis Group

NEW YORK AND LONDON

Designed cover image: Jennifer Strezo

First published 2025
by Routledge
605 Third Avenue, New York, NY 10158

and by Routledge
4 Park Square, Milton Park, Abingdon, Oxon, OX14 4RN

*Routledge is an imprint of the Taylor & Francis Group, an informa
business*

ISBN: 978-1-032-59657-0 (hbk)
ISBN: 978-1-032-59652-5 (pbk)
ISBN: 978-1-003-45561-5 (ebk)

DOI: 10.4324/9781003455615

Typeset in Sabon
by Apex CoVantage, LLC

Contents

About the author

Natsuyo N. Lipschutz, CSP, MBA, is an international keynote speaker and cross-cultural communication specialist. Natsuyo co-authored *The Success Blueprint*, along with world-renowned business speaker Brian Tracy. She is also the award-winning author of *20Ji Ni Sogiotose* (*Say It in 20 Words*) in Japanese, Korean, and Chinese, as well as *Story ni otoshikome* (*Motivate with Your Own Story*) in Japanese and Chinese. *20Ji Ni Sogiotose* was awarded "the top 10 business books of the year" in 2021.

Natsuyo is also an engaging TEDx speaker, a five-time Toastmasters International speech contest champion, a world-class certified public speaking coach, and a U.S.–Asia business strategy consultant.

Using a multilayered approach of cross-cultural communication skills, logical thinking frameworks, and storytelling techniques, Natsuyo assists global organizations to improve cultural diversity and have their leaders communicate effectively beyond differences so they can get their messages not only clearly heard, but also acted upon across cultures.

Natsuyo began her career at a top Japanese trading company, ITOCHU International, in New York. Natsuyo then received her MBA from New York University and held a management consultant internship position at McKinsey & Company. Today, Natsuyo is the managing principal of her strategy consulting firm, ASPIRE Intelligence, as well as an executive consultant for Breakthrough Speaking, a global public speaking consultancy.

From 2021 to 2024, Natsuyo also served as the first Asian board director at the National Speakers Association New York City chapter (NSANYC), and a recipient of the 2023 NSANYC member of the year award. In 2024, she became the first Japanese person receive the Certified Speaking Professional (CSP®) designation.

In addition to her dynamic speaking and consulting career, Natsuyo is a competitive ballroom Latin dance national finalist, a proud mother, and a cancer survivor.

Websites

- Professional speaker website (ENG): www.natsuyolipschutz.us
- ASPIRE intelligence website (ENG, JP): www.aspireintelligence.com
- Breakthrough Speaking (JP): www.btspeaking.com
- E-learning course: https://natsuyo-s-school.thinkific.com

Social media

- LinkedIn: www.linkedin.com/in/natsuyolipschutz/
- Instagram: www.instagram.com/natsuyo_lipschutz/
- YouTube: www.youtube.com/c/BreakthroughSpeaking

Introduction

In the fall of 1993, I was 21 years old and a junior in college in Japan. One day, I saw a flyer about a one-year exchange program to the United States of America.

The flyer displayed a beautiful campus, happy students, and lots of sunshine.

Looking over the details, I said to myself, *this is my bright future! Here I come, the Sunshine State! St. Louis Missouri . . . !*

Wait a minute . . . . Show Me the Sunshine . . .

In case you are not familiar with state nicknames in the United States, it turned out that the Sunshine State is actually Florida; Missouri is the Show Me State. I didn't know that I got them mixed up until I made this joke to someone from St. Louis years later!! Talk about a cultural misunderstanding . . .

Fast forward through paperwork, tests, interviews, and a 17-hour flight to Day 1 of the exchange program in St. Louis. I attended the student-led campus tour. The student tour guide was tall, muscular, and resembled Tom Cruise.

"Tom Cruise" was wearing a T-Shirt and a hat, both featuring a red bird and the word *Cardinals*.

Cardinals, I thought to myself. *Huh, interesting . . . "Tom Cruise" must . . . love . . . birds.*

"Hey," he greeted me with a big toothy smile. "Waz up?"

"Up . . . ?"

I literally looked up in the sky in response to his question. But there was absolutely nothing in the sky. *Am I missing something? Is it the red bird he loves? I can't find it. Why would he trick me like that? "Tom Cruise" sure is a peculiar guy . . .*

DOI: 10.4324/9781003455615-1

The group of girls on the tour started speaking excitedly in English to each other and gesturing in my direction. "O. M. G. Seriously?! No, she didn't! I can't even!!!"

What's OMG? Is that a secret code I'm supposed to open a door with? Oh, is it what's "up" there? I wondered with increasing anxiety. *Can't even what?* Why couldn't the girls finish their sentences, like I learned on my English textbook? And to make things worse, they were speaking so, so fast!

I was lost. I felt different. I felt disconnected . . .

One Friday night, my dorm hosted a party.

Blasting music, beer bottles, pizza boxes all over the place. And drunk Americans talked even faster!

I decided this was the last place I wanted to be, and started to make a stealthy exit. I almost managed my way through the crowd, trying to rush back to my room. But someone blocked my way.

It was Nate. A surfer dude, long brown hair, and sunglasses. Think *The Big Lebowski.*

Really?! Sunglasses at night?! Only a surfer dude in land-locked Missouri.

Nate came up to me, grabbed my shoulder and said, "Dude, don't be so anti-social!!"

That was a verbal knife to me.

I was struggling to assimilate. I couldn't talk like them, act like them, think like them. I couldn't even understand them. My frustration was at its peak. I felt like a water filled balloon, ready to explode. And this surfer dude popped it.

Overwhelmed, I burst into tears in front of everyone. What a party spoiler. I hated myself even more. I uttered something in Japanese.

"Dude . . . !???" Nate asked

Then I tried to squeeze out my last bit of courage, and put my English words together.

"I can't speak English well!!"

Then, Nate gave me words of wisdom that changed my life.

"Yeah . . . and . . . ?"

He didn't care that my English was broken. He didn't care I looked different. He didn't care I was from a totally different culture. And I realized I was the one – the only one – refusing to embrace the differences.

Regardless of what you experience with people, *you* need to embrace the differences and adapt. You can't just do things in your old ways, wait, and expect others to compromise for you.

The last thing I expected was to get enlightened by a surfer dude. But his two magical words (and maybe something about the sunglasses too?) brought me back the right attitude: **Yes, AND.**

You may have heard of the concept of "Yes, AND."

"Yes, AND" is often used in the improv world. It encourages you to listen and be receptive to other's ideas. Rather than immediately judging the idea, you accept it *and* build upon it. "Yes, AND" gives you an open-minded mindset to embrace differences and bring out improved results.

A few days later, I decided to open up my door. Literally. Whenever I was in my dorm room, I kept the door open. People popped in and said "Hi, y'all!"

Yes, AND, I decided that I'll have a few words with them, instead of just saying hi.

Yes, AND, I decided I'm going to knock on their doors time to time, and have a little chat.

Fast forward 30 years and look at me now, *dude*! I'm a cross-cultural communication specialist and a professional speaker, and I work with leading global companies and their leaders to help them communicate effectively beyond differences. If you hear my keynote speeches, you may still detect a trace of Japanese accent, but . . . Yes, AND?

* * *

Perhaps your cross-cultural journey may be different. You may face "differences" with your overseas clients or culturally diverse team, or with different departments, different generations, different personalities . . . .

If you're a multilingual, multicultural global business leader, or any kind of leader who needs to communicate with, present to, or persuade diverse counterparts/stakeholders, I wrote this book for you. My hope is to help you develop and deliver your one-of-a-kind message powerfully, persuasively, and authentically, so that your audience clearly understands you *and then takes action.*

One important principle to remember is that you want to be **curious** about each other's differences, and have a "Yes, AND" mindset.

With this mindset, we will explore the 3-Step Process called "The 3As" so that you can clearly communicate to understand, and be understood.

Illustration of the iceberg model

A little bit about me.

I was born and raised in Japan. At college, I studied Chinese and French while majoring in business communications. While in college, I spent one month in Sydney, Australia, and one year in St. Louis, Missouri. When I landed my first job in New York, I immigrated to the United States. I married a Jewish dentist from Philadelphia. I earned my MBA from New York University. By that time, I had visited approximately 20 countries for business and pleasure. Oh, and I have been an avid competitive Latin dancer, and I have competed throughout the United States and in Europe with my Russian dance partner. My books so far have been written in Japanese, English, Chinese, and Korean. All of these are so appropriate, since my work is cross-culture, right?

Since I immigrated to the United States in 1995, I went through three phases in my career.

The first phase is when I worked for a Japanese company in New York, mainly dealing with non-Japanese clients. I was still "quite Japanese" back then, experienced a big cultural gap with Americans, and made many communication mistakes.

The second phase is when I started my own consulting firm, and most of my clients were Japanese companies in Japan. I evolved to be more "Americanized" and experienced a *big* cultural gap with Japanese, and made many communication mistakes.

The third phase is now. Besides my strategy consulting business, I also have a global public speaking business. My clients are now diverse, and I am teaching global leaders effective cross-cultural communication skills.

When I say cross-cultural communications, however, I am *not only* talking about cross-country. Culture is like an onion . . . multilayered. When you have different values, different ways of thinking or doing things, you form a unique culture. So I am talking about cross-functional, cross-department, cross-regional, cross-occupational . . . . All of that. Even if you are from the same country or region, your culture and communication style could be very unique.

What makes you successful in your culture doesn't make you successful in their culture. To become an effective leader and communicator in global business, we must be able to break through cultural *and* personal barriers. If cultural diversity is managed well, powerful team synergies arise. But, when it's not managed well, your business could fall apart. I know it first hand, because I've been there.

Before we take a deep dive into cross-cultural communication, let me share with you how I came up with the 3As.

As I said earlier, I'm a strategy consultant and professional speaker, but also a competitive ballroom Latin dancer.

Have you ever seen the TV show *Dancing with the Stars* or the movie *Shall We Dance?* That's what I do!

To be a bit technical, the mainstream competition style of Latin dancing is called International Latin, and it consists of five distinct dances – Chacha, Samba, Rumba, Paso Doble, and Jive. As a competitor, you need to dance all five dances back-to-back, approximately 1.5 minutes each, with 15 seconds or so in between to catch your breath. It's like running a sprint five times in a row. That's why it's called a "Dance Sport."

International Latin dance on the competition floor is a thrilling and visually stunning display of talent, athleticism, and artistry. Approximately ten couples dance on the floor all at the same time. So you need to pay close attention to your surroundings as well as your partner, so you can move in sync without disturbing or being disturbed by other couples, while maintaining precise foot work, intricate partnering, expressive body movements, interaction with audience, and storytelling with every language you've got except verbal language.

What's Latin dancing got to do with cross-cultural communication?

Well, the 3-Step Process called "The 3As" I developed was actually inspired by my experience as a Latin dancer.

Competitive Latin dancing is a very interactive partnership dance. It is closely intertwined with communication.

Let me explain.

- **Partnership:** Competitive Latin dancing is performed as a couple. Two dancers must establish and maintain a clear and effective line of communication with each other throughout the performance. This communication is all conveyed non-verbally, of course, and it is essential for synchronizing movements, coordinating timing, and maintaining physical connection. It involves eye contact, body language, and breath, so a mutual understanding of each other's intentions and actions can be effectively established.
- **Lead and follow:** In Latin dance, there is a clear division of roles – one dancer is a leader, and the other a follower. A leader takes the lead in initiating movements and a follower catches subtle signs of the leader, adjusts movements accordingly, and follows the lead. Effective communication between the lead and follow is crucial for a successful performance. The lead must communicate their intentions and signals clearly, while the follow must interpret and respond to those signals accurately. This communication allows for seamless transitions, synchronized footwork, and coordinated body movements.
- **Musicality:** Competitive Latin dancers must have a strong sense of musicality which involves understanding and interpreting the rhythm, tempo, and nuances of the music. They communicate their understanding of the music through their movements, accentuating certain beats and expressing the character and emotions of the music. This ability to communicate and connect with the music enhances the overall performance and captivates the audience.
- **Expression and emotion:** Competitive Latin dancing goes beyond technical proficiency. It requires dancers to convey emotion, passion, and the essence of the dance through their expressions and body language. It is a nonverbal form of storytelling. Dancers need to communicate the vivid story to the audience and judges, evoking emotions and telling a story through movement. Dancers must communicate their intent and the narrative of the dance clearly to engage and captivate the viewers. Just imagine: How interesting can dancing be if it's all about precise movements with deadpan face?
- **Performance and connection with the audience:** Competitive Latin dancing involves not only communication within the partnership but also communication with the audience. Dancers aim to establish a connection with the spectators, drawing them into their performance and

eliciting an emotional response. This connection is created through eye contact, facial expressions, and projecting their energy and emotions toward the audience. Sometimes it's playful. Sometimes seductive. It allows dancers to effectively communicate their artistic interpretation and create a memorable and engaging performance.

Competitive Latin dancing requires effective communication at various levels – between partners, with the music, and with the audience. It involves nonverbal cues, body language, musical interpretation, and emotional expression. The ability to communicate clearly and skillfully enhances the dancers' performance, creates a captivating experience, and allows them to convey their artistic vision and connection to the audience.

All of these communication techniques of competitive Latin dancers can be summarized into the 3As. And I took my lessons from the ballroom to the boardroom, and am convinced that cross-cultural communication goes the same way.

If you are thinking, *uh oh, I'm not a dancer* . . . don't worry, you don't have to start taking dance lessons in order to become a better cross-cultural communicator!

Then, is there something I can do to learn effective cross-cultural communication?

Yes, AND we will learn it "step by step."

Let's dive in.

Chapter 1

Why isn't it getting through?

Scores and terminology of "The Country Comparison Tool" were updated on October 2023 by The Culture Factor group, www.hofstede-insights.com by Hofstede Insights Oy, Business ID 1652415-9

Meet Bill. Bill worked for a large American apparel wholesale company, and his company wanted to expand to the Japanese market. Bill was one of the top salespeople, and he was in charge of Asia Pacific. Originally from the U.S. Midwest, in his mid-40's, very outgoing with a great sense of humor. He had this stoic characteristic about him, and he was called "the closer" by his peers.

His company just set the mid-term strategy that Japan would be the gateway to their market expansion in Asia Pacific, and Bill the closer was sent to Japan to meet with leading Japanese retailers.

Bill was prepared. He researched market trends in Japan. He identified one product category that would be a sure win in the Japanese market. He put together colorful presentation materials with many pictures of their products, price lists, and order forms. All he had to do was to present as Bill the closer always does with his charm, but just speak slightly slower than usual. That's all.

The meeting with one of the largest Japanese retailers went successfully. He had delivered his presentation to the Japanese manager and his assistant just like he planned, and they had listened carefully, nodded in agreement, liked the product photos, and asked no questions.

My gosh, not a single question! I must have been so crystal clear with everything I said, because I deliberately spoke slower. Bill thought.

Taking all these reactions as a positive sign, Bill handed them the order form at the end of the meeting with great confidence. The Japanese retailer accepted the order form and said, "It all looks great. Thank you." He made a receiving gesture and bowed.

As soon as Bill came back to the United States, he went straight to his boss and said, "Boss! We got the order!" All seemed well.

But . . . a month went by but no order form. Another month went by. Still nothing.

That's when Bill called me. "The meeting went very well," he said. "Why haven't they submitted their order? Can you find out?"

DOI: 10.4324/9781003455615-2

I conducted detailed market research and analysis for Bill's company – primary research and secondary research to collect data about the industry trends, market drivers, competitive landscapes, consumer behavior . . . and analyzed and interpreted data to derive meaningful insights. However, I didn't find anything that far off from what Bill had researched.

I further polished his presentation materials, and this time, I flew to Japan to meet with the Japanese retailer.

I started off by saying,

"I know you met with Bill a few months ago. How did the meeting go?"

"It was good!" the manager answered.

"It was good?"

"Yes," he confirmed. "Mr. Bill was a nice person."

There. *This is exactly where the discrepancy happened*, I thought to myself. In light of this information, I needed to ask some questions.

"Do you think Bill's products fit into your existing product portfolio?"

"Yes, they would."

"Is the price point within a range?"

"I think so."

"Their lead time is one month. Does it work for you?"

"Absolutely."

Ok, this isn't going where I want to go, I thought. I pivoted my questioning approach. I switched to "open-ended" and *GOOD* questions, from "closed-ended" and "Light" questions. (Don't worry, I will explain these in Chapter 5.)

"Are there different requirements and processes for a new vendor to open an account with you?"

"What are the potential roadblocks, if any, that might stand in our way?"

"What does it take for a new foreign vendor to close a deal?"

The retailer looked down and said, "Ooooh, no, no, we are not ready to order from a new vendor . . . especially a foreign vendor. But Mr. Bill came all the way from the U.S. to meet with us, and his products were very nice. We wanted to be at least polite in case a potential opportunity might come up in the future."

Bingo. Truth came out. If I didn't ask strategic questions, this conversation would have gone south.

The retailer was not planning to place an order. They had made their decision before Bill even presented. So not only did Bill fail to make sales, he lost credibility in his company.

Bill had completely misinterpreted what he thought he was seeing and hearing. Why? Because he didn't understand the effective cross-cultural communication process that I call "the 3As."

In a cross-cultural situation, when you apply your own familiar "*Why*" to judge "*What*" you see or hear, you take in the wrong message and create a huge misunderstanding just like Bill had.

But Bill isn't alone. Every year organizations lose money, time, and people due to this kind of poor or inefficient cross-cultural communication. The good news, fortunately, is that people can learn the skills necessary to prevent these issues.

If you are thinking, *My company isn't global* or *My business doesn't deal with overseas, so cross-cultural communication doesn't really apply to me*, let me challenge you.

Culture of One

Let's think about "cross-culture" for a moment.

If you were to explain "what culture is" to third graders, how would you describe it?

Take a piece of paper, pause, and draw a picture of what you think best describes "culture."

Pause

I'm not the best artist in the world, so I'm glad this is not a live TV where I have to show my artwork. But if I were to draw a picture, I would draw an onion. Yes, an onion!

To me, "culture" is multilayered, like an onion.

Explanation of Culture of One

When you look at it, the first thing you see is the outer layer of the onion – that's the national difference – I'm Japanese. That's what you see first when we meet.

But if you peel off that layer, underneath lies many other layers of elements that have influenced your value system – like an onion – such as the region or city where you had lived, the school you went to, your family and friends, the company you work for, and more . . .

Cross-cultural difference is not just about country and country difference. Think for example about the East Coast and the West Coast of the United States. Think about the sales department and the finance department in your company. Think about you and your neighbor across the street!

I may have a "Japanese" look outside, but I've been living in the United States for almost half of my life, and all of my professional life. My values, attitudes, behavioral patterns, thought process, demeanor, communication styles, and common sense are not those of "typical" Japanese.

What is typical, anyway?

The No. 1 thing that stands between you and your culturally diverse audience is "common sense."

Over the years, we built up our own set of "common sense" that had been cultivated by layers of onion.

Imagine that you are wearing layers of onion as your glasses.

Picture of author wearing layers of glasses

And this is how we look at your world.

This becomes our common sense.

As we grow up in our own bubble, we start to look at things through *our* lenses and decide our views are "common sense." However, *in cross-cultural situations, your common sense may not be so common.*

We need to remove our layers of common sense, assumptions, unwritten rules, or our way of how things are done, and embrace and celebrate our differences! That's true diversity. Right? The only way to do that is to dig deeper into uncovering the "Culture of One."

When you have different values and different ways of thinking or doing things, you form your own unique culture. You may be from the same country or even neighborhood, but "your culture and communication style" could still be different. At the end of the day, we all have different values, opinions, or communication styles. We are all uniquely different. And we all form our own unique culture.

That's the Culture of One.

So we *all* need to tap into this Culture of One and acquire effective cross-cultural communication skills. If we don't, communication mistakes could happen with someone sitting right next to you.

Then, how can we remove our lenses and communicate effectively beyond our differences?

The 3As.

The first "A" is Acknowledge.

Illustration of the iceberg model

Acknowledge: culture as an iceberg

In the cross-cultural field, culture is often described as an iceberg.[1]

Illustration of the iceberg model

Let's say that you are sitting on a boat, looking at it.

Can you see the entire figure all the way to the bottom? No.

You only see the tip of the iceberg, right?

But there is a much, much larger piece hiding under the surface, that's supporting the tip of the iceberg.

That's what the culture looks like.

You can see *What* they look like and hear *What* they say, but that's only the tip of the iceberg.

Why they say what they say, and *Why* they do what they do, are all hiding under the surface.

And when you don't know what's hiding under the surface . . . you could cause a deadly Titanic moment. Even between people you think would share the same culture.

Let me take you back to 2005, soon after I started my own strategy consulting firm in New York.

I was hired by Mr. Nakano. Mr. Nakano was a 65-year-old retired government official who then became the chairman of a 400-year-old Japanese craft company. The company produced Samurai swords.

Mr. Nakano was very experienced, and he had his strategy all laid out. But he had just been transferred to the United States to start their New York office. He wanted to make sure that his strategy was going to work in the United States.

One day, he called me over and said,

信元さん、あなたにお願いすることにしたからしっかり頼んだよ。

That means, "You are hired!"

By that time, I had been in the United States for 10 years already. I became American enough to understand how things work over here, yet I was Japanese enough to understand how things work over there.

Little did I know that I still needed to learn how to bridge our differences.

Have you ever made a small communication mistake but you didn't know you did, and lost something big?

As soon as Mr. Nakano hired me, I conducted extensive research and analysis, as I always do as a strategy consultant, then I said to myself:

Uh oh. His strategy is going to take forever! We need a shortcut to get into the market quickly. Forget his strategy. I know the market! How do I tell him though . . . . Well, if I explain the new strategy in detail, he would agree with me. After all, he hired me to conduct business in an American way. No problem!!

Problem!

As a young, aspiring strategy consultant, I was so driven with my mission. *I'm going to take this company to great success in the United States*, I told myself. So what did I do? I put together a very detailed presentation, explaining why Mr. Nakano's strategy wouldn't work, and why mine would.

Very logical. No room for argument. I was so confident that Mr. Nakano would thank me.

I attached my masterpiece presentation in e-mail, put Mr. Nakano in the recipient's field, and cc'd everybody – the president, the COO, the marketing manager, the production manager, and even their assistants.

Now what do you think happened?

Next day, I received the shortest e-mail from Mr. Nakano. Just two words.

Call me.

I said two words to myself.

Oh yeah!

He must have loved my proposed strategy and couldn't wait to discuss more.

I called him right away. Then he gave me another two words.

Come today.

. . . I think he REALLY LOVES my strategy!!!

If you came with me later that day, you would have found Mr. Nakano sitting behind his antique desk by the window. He directed me to sit at a sofa closer to the door. (This is a subtle nuance of "power distance" in Japanese culture, where the higher-ranked person sits the farthest from the door, and a lower-ranked person sits closest to the door.) On the wall hangs a beautiful shiny Samurai sword above his shiny bald head.

"What a shiny masterpiece . . . !" I uttered. I mean, the sword!

While looking out the window with Park Avenue stretching in front of him, his voice cut through the air.

"Who do you think you are?!"

I said,

"Well, I'm your consultant, you hired me," I said. And in my head: *Who do you think* you *are?*

. . . . In my head.

Then he slowly rises, and grabs the sword.

Oh no! I thought, sitting up. *What am I going to fight him with??*

Instead of fighting, he told me a story.

Four hundred years ago when our company was founded, there were several Samurai sword makers in the area. Most of them learned to mass produce swords, and made them available to the rich and the poor, the young and the old, from the north to the south. But our founder, Yushichi, insisted on the most painstaking way of making swords. It took three to four weeks to make one sword. But that's how you make a masterpiece.

Now, we are the only company that's still standing.

To make a masterpiece, you must master the pieces.

No shortcut!!

Your strategy was all about taking the shortcut. I don't need efficiency. I need a masterpiece.

Before I could say anything, he gave me two more words that I will never forget: "*You're fired.*"

In just a few months, I went from "You're hired" to "You're fired."

What happened??

Thinking back, Mr. Nakano kept giving me two words . . . You're hired. Call me. Come today. You're fired.

Those are *What* I heard. But I was only scratching the tip of the iceberg.
I completely misconstrued what I *thought* he was saying. Why?
Because I didn't understand there was more hiding under the surface.
So Why did he say what he said?
He was probably thinking,
You're hired – because I need you to reassure my team that *my* strategy is correct.
Call me and *come today* – because we need to talk privately about what you did wrong.
You're fired – because you embarrassed me in front of my team. You don't know your place.
You are disrespectful.
You're fired.
That's the *Why* – the rest of the iceberg I totally missed seeing.

In a cross-cultural situation, we face differences in values, opinions, perspectives, or communication styles. And yet we often apply our own familiar "*Why*" to judge "*What*" we see or hear. But this would cause a huge misunderstanding, miscommunication, and mistrust.

Just like I did – and Bill did, too.

When Bill delivered his presentation to the Japanese retailers, they listened carefully, nodded, liked the product photos, and asked no questions. Bill applied his familiar "*Why*" to judge the "*What*."

"What" Bill saw → Bill's "Why"

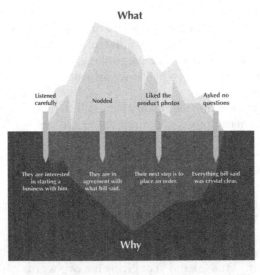

Explanation of what Bill heard and his why

WhatHAT" Bill saw → Bill's "WhyHY"

- Listened carefully → They are interested in starting a business with him.
- Nodded → They were in agreement with what Bill said.
- Liked the product photos → Their next step is to place an order.
- Asked no questions → Everything Bill said was crystal clear.

However, the Japanese retailer's "Why" were quite different.

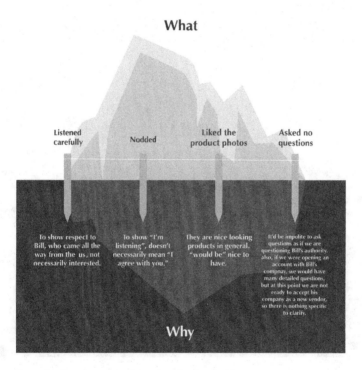

"What" Bill saw ➝ Japanese's "Why"

What

| Listened carefully | Nodded | Liked the product photos | Asked no questions |

To show respect to Bill, who came all the way from the us, not necessarily interested.

To show "I'm listening", doesn't necessarily mean "I agree with you."

They are nice looking products in general. "would be" nice to have.

It'd be impolite to ask questions as if we are questioning Bill's authority. also, if we were opening an account with Bill's compnay, we would have many detailed questions, but at this point we are not ready to accept his company as a new vendor, so there is nothing specific to clarify.

Why

Explanation of what Japanese heard and why

As you can see, the first and most important step of the 3As is to Acknowledge that your iceberg, especially the hidden "Why" part of the iceberg, might look quite different from theirs.

Now, here is a challenge question for you.

Are you open-minded enough to Acknowledge that your common sense may not be common?

Remember, in a cross-cultural situation, your common sense may not be so common. And effective cross-cultural communication starts with a little curiosity and open-mindedness to Acknowledge different icebergs – especially the parts you can't see.

Analyze

When you Acknowledge the difference, our second step is to Analyze where your communication gap lies, and how big the gap is, digging deeper into the part of the iceberg you can't see.

Let's say you just proposed some action plans to your boss, and your boss says this to you.

"*That's difficult.*"

How would you interpret this?

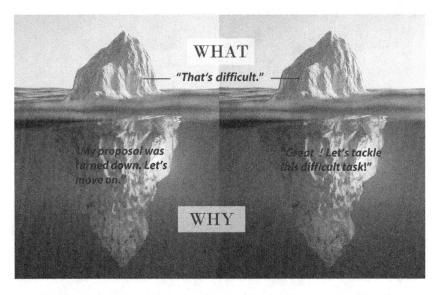

Example of miscommunication using the iceberg model

If you are from Japan, like myself, everyone knows this means a clear "No." Your proposal was just turned down. But if you are from Switzerland or Germany, you may think "great! I just proposed a challenging task!" You may even continue to think, "if I can overcome this challenge, I'm going to get promoted!"

What a huge gap in interpretation, right? This happens quite often. What if you had that Japanese boss and you spent all of your time working on it for the next few weeks, when your Japanese boss wanted you to use your time for something "better"? You are not going to get promotion. You'll get demotion!!

We want to avoid such a costly mistake, yes?

We just learned that the first step to approach cross-culture is to Acknowledge that they may have a different iceberg. In this case, "That's difficult" might have a different underlined meaning to it.

Now, the second step. Analyze.

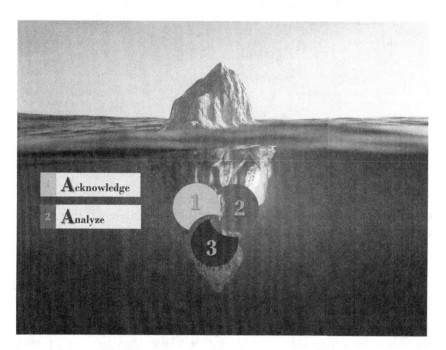

Illustration of the iceberg model

Let me introduce you to two famous cross-cultural models to help you analyze effectively.

High Context–Low Context

The first tool is one of the most famous cross-cultural tools, High Context– Low Context.[2]

It was introduced by an anthropologist, Edward T. Hall.

Hall examined the factors that influence intercultural understanding and thus enhance or impede communication between individuals from different cultural backgrounds. His work led him to formulate a cultural dimension called context. Context explains the way people evaluate and interpret the meaning of information that they receive.[3]

LOW Context Culture of "Verbal Messages"	HIGH Context Culture of "Inferences"
<Communication tendencies> Direct Emphasis on verbal Explicit "I" focused Risk takers Interpreted at face value Relationships begin and end quickly Disagreement is depersonalized Result-oriented Fast with change	<Communication tendencies> Indirect Emphasis on non-verbal Implicit "We" focused Risk-averse Read between the lines Relationships build slowly Sensitive to conflict Process-oriented Slow with change

Illustration of High Context and Low Context model

According to Hall, our communication styles are categorized into two types: High Context and Low Context, or culture of inferences (High Context culture), and culture of verbal messages (Low Context culture).[4]

In a High Context culture, people rely on surroundings and environment. It's not necessary, and can even be inappropriate, to spell everything out too explicitly. So a listener knows to read between the lines – the "context" hiding under the surface.[5] In Japanese, we say "ku-ki wo yomu," or, "read the atmosphere."

High Context people "read the atmosphere" and make their own conclusions to understand the context, so that relationship, harmony, power balance, and security are all maintained within a team.

On the other hand, in a Low Context culture, verbal messages are received at face value, leaving no room for inferences. They are more explicit, logical, and direct, which means "Tell what you are going to tell, then tell them, then tell them what you've told them."[6]

Low Context people focus more on individual excellence, rather than group harmony.

And this is typically what happens between High Context and Low Context.

Low Context people would be thinking,

Why don't you say what you mean?! If you meant differently, you should have verbalized it. So if there was any misunderstanding, it's not my fault. Why didn't you say it?

And they may just say this straight to your face.

But High Context people would be thinking,

Why do I have to spell everything out? Get the nuances! Read the atmosphere and understand what it really means! Don't make me say it!

And this context is most likely hiding in the part of the iceberg you don't see.

So when you only see the tip of the iceberg, and you don't consider what the entire figure looks like, you could create a deadly Titanic moment . . . like me, with Mr. Nakano.

Now, remember Mr. Nakano kept giving me two words?

His communication style relies on "context" . . . which makes him *very* High Context. He thought he conveyed his intention clearly, but there was huge room for misinterpretation. I would have interpreted it correctly, *if* I shared the same context. However, I took his word only superficially, added in my own interpretation (a *wrong* one), and thought he was excited about my proposal.

What does that make me?

Low Context.

I took his words at their face value, *and* I communicated my strategy in such detail, a strategy which was against Mr. Nakano's plan. I spelled everything out clearly, explicitly, and logically. On top of that, I cc'd everybody to be super transparent.

Very Low Context.

What about Bill's case?

The Japanese retailer didn't say much, relying for their communication more on context, which means High Context. On the other hand, Bill presented his materials explicitly, or in a Low Context way. From Bill's Low Context point of view, if nothing was voiced or questioned, that means everything is clearly understood, and they have nothing more to add. However, apparently, the Japanese had a lot more in the context. If Bill had known the High Context–Low Context model, he would have noticed that there was a gap, but he still hasn't learned how to close that gap . . . which we will soon learn in step 3 of the 3As.

This country mapping might be helpful to decode what happened. Remember, I've been in the United States for a while, so even though I'm Japanese, my communication style is more like an American's.

Expected influence on the adoption of innovations

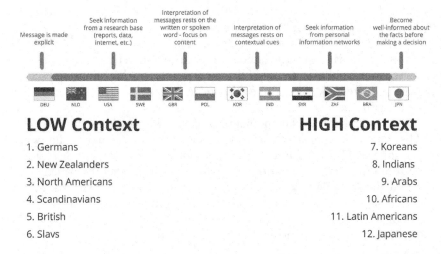

LOW Context	HIGH Context
1. Germans	7. Koreans
2. New Zealanders	8. Indians
3. North Americans	9. Arabs
4. Scandinavians	10. Africans
5. British	11. Latin Americans
6. Slavs	12. Japanese

Ilustration of High Context and Low Context distribution by countries

Dimensions of National Culture

The second tool I'd like to introduce you to is called the "Dimensions of National Culture"[7] by Geert Hofstede.

Hofstede is a Dutch social psychologist. He conducted research on IBM employees in 60 countries around the world, and studied how values in the workplace are influenced by culture. Hofstede's model is considered one of the most comprehensive cross-cultural studies to examine cultural differences and their impact on organizational behavior. His research resulted in identifying six cultural dimensions that help in understanding how values and behaviors vary across different national cultures.

Individualism
"I" focused

Collectivism
"We" focused

LOW Uncertainty Avoidance
Risk tolerant

Uncertainty Avoidance HIGH
Risk averse

LOW Power Distance
Egalitarian

Power Distance HIGH
Hierarchical

Masculine
Power important

Feminine
Nurture & harmony important

Short-Term Orientation
Immediate result

Long-Term Orientation
Futuristic

Indulgence
Satisfaction is good

Restraint
Normative repression

Illustration of Hofstede's cultural dimensions

These dimensions are as follows. Since this framework has six indexes and could get quite complex, I'll start with a definition of each index along with general examples, then dig deeper by comparing different cultures.

1. Individualism vs. collectivism

This scale measures the degree to which individuals are integrated into groups.

In individualistic cultures, the emphasis is put on personal achievements and individual rights. People are expected to stand up for themselves and their immediate family, and to choose their own affiliations. I call this individualistic tendency, the "I-Focused." In contrast, in collectivist cultures, people often act as a part of a group. They put a group before an individual, and group harmony is important to them. People may have large extended families, which are used as protection in exchange for loyalty. I call this collective tendency, the "We-Focused." For example:

Imagine you as a team leader want collaborative teamwork from your team members. If you say to them, "let's work hard together as a team," it may resonate with people from collective cultures, because they immediately feel that "as part of this team, we all must put in our best effort." But for people from individualistic cultures, their motivation has to be directly tied to their personal goals, so you might adjust your message to something like this: "Our overall team result will be directly reflected on your year-end evaluation." Then, your message becomes "I-Focused," which will resonate more with the individualistic culture.

2. Uncertainty avoidance – high vs. low

This scale measures the extent to which the members of a culture feel threatened by ambiguous or unknown situations.

Uncertainty avoidance *high* cultures need predictability. They need written as well as unwritten rules to make sure that nothing is a surprise. For these people, uncertainty or risk is a cause of anxiety, so they try to minimize unusual circumstances and proceed with careful changes step by step by implementing rules, laws, and regulations. In contrast, uncertainty avoidance *low* cultures accept and feel comfortable in unstructured situations or various changes, and try to have as few rules as possible. Go with the flow attitude. For example:

In an uncertainty avoidance *high* culture, contract negotiations tend to be thorough and detailed. Parties involved seek to include as many provisions as possible to anticipate potential uncertainties and minimize risks. The contract is likely to include strict deadlines, penalties for non-compliance, and precise specifications to ensure that there is little room for ambiguity or unexpected events.

In contrast, in an uncertainty avoidance *low* culture, contract negotiations may be more relaxed and flexible. Parties focus on establishing a basic framework and trust, allowing for more open-ended agreements. The contract is seen as a starting point, subject to potential revisions and modifications throughout the business relationship.

3. Power distance

Power distance is the extent to which the less powerful members of the group accept and expect that power is distributed unequally.

Cultures with *low* power distance expect and accept power relations are more consultative or democratic. For example:

Power distance *high* cultures may emphasize a hierarchical structure and a more top-down decision-making process. They expect decisions to be made by higher-level management and adhere to a more formal communication style, which involves multiple layers to go through. You need to climb up levels one at a time to get to the top decision maker.

In contrast, members of power distance *low* culture may have a flat organizational structure and an egalitarian approach to decision-making. They express their ideas openly and expect an equal opportunity to contribute to the decision-making process. They value a collaborative environment where opinions are heard, regardless of seniority.

4. Masculinity vs. femininity

This dimension reflects the degree to which a society values traditionally masculine or feminine traits. Cultures with high masculinity place importance on competition, assertiveness, and achievement, while cultures with high femininity prioritize nurturing, collaboration, and quality of life. For example:

Gender roles tend to be more distinct in the masculine culture, with men expected to be assertive, ambitious, and focused on career advancement. The society values assertiveness, toughness, and individual achievement. Work–life balance may lean towards work, and there might be a preference for a hierarchical organizational structure. In contrast, in a culture characterized by high femininity, collaboration, care, and quality of life are prioritized. Gender roles are more fluid, and both men and women are encouraged to display nurturing, empathetic, and relationship-oriented qualities. The society values cooperation, consensus-building, and maintaining a harmonious work environment. Work–life balance is emphasized, and there might be a preference for a more egalitarian organizational structure.

5. Long-term orientation vs. short-term orientation

This dimension examines the extent to which a society emphasizes long-term planning and values persistence, perseverance, and thriftiness. Cultures with long-term orientation value traditions, savings, and investing in the future. Conversely, cultures with short-term orientation focus on the present, immediate gratification, and fulfilling social obligations. For example:

In a culture characterized by a long-term orientation, individuals tend to prioritize future rewards, persistence, and perseverance. They value traditions, thriftiness, and investing in education and preparation for the long run. There is a focus on delayed gratification and a willingness to sacrifice immediate gains for future benefits. Planning for the future, building long-lasting relationships, and respecting authority and social norms are highly valued.

In contrast, in a culture characterized by a short-term orientation, individuals are more inclined to focus on immediate outcomes, quick results, and fulfilling present needs and desires. They value spontaneity, adaptability, and enjoying the present moment. There may be a lesser emphasis on long-term planning and a preference for instant gratification and flexible approaches to work and life. Experimentation, innovation, and risk-taking are encouraged, as the emphasis is on seizing opportunities in the present rather than considering long-term consequences.

6. Indulgence vs. restraint

This dimension reflects the extent to which a society allows gratification of natural human desires and impulses. Indulgent cultures tend to emphasize enjoyment, leisure, and personal fulfillment, while restrained cultures promote self-control, strict social norms, and suppression of gratification. For example:

In a culture characterized by high indulgence, there is a greater acceptance and encouragement of gratifying basic human desires and enjoying life's pleasures. Individuals prioritize personal happiness, self-expression, and pursuing personal interests and passions. There is a lenient attitude toward indulging in leisure activities, entertainment, and satisfying immediate needs and desires. Society promotes individual freedom and self-fulfillment, allowing for more relaxed social norms and a higher tolerance for diverse lifestyles and behaviors.

In contrast, in a culture characterized by high restraint, there is a stronger emphasis on self-discipline, self-control, and suppressing immediate gratification for the sake of societal or long-term goals. Individuals prioritize duty, responsibility, and adherence to social norms and rules. There is a focus on maintaining order, modesty, and adhering to traditional values. The society promotes a more regulated and structured lifestyle, whereby individuals exercise restraint and avoid excessive indulgence or displays of personal desires.

These country mapping are not a complete mapping, but it may be interesting in learning each country's general tendencies.

	High score means	Low score means
Individualism / Collectivism	More collectivism	More individualism
Uncertainty avoidance	More risk averse	More risk tolerant
Power distance	More hierarchical	More egalitarian
Femininity / Masculinity	More masculine	More feminine
Long-term vs. short- term orientations	More long-term	More short-term
Indulgence vs. restraint	More indulgent	More restraint

Explanation of scoring in Hofstede's Cultural Dimensions

Source: Data from "Country Comparison Tool," The Culture Factor, accessed August 2023, https://www.hofstede-insights.com/country-comparison-tool. License for use granted by The Culture Factor Group – Hofstede Insights Oy.

Analyze with these tools

One important thing you need to keep in mind.

In both High Context–Low Context and Dimensions of National Culture, general rule of thumb is that Western cultures often tend to be more Low Context, individualistic, uncertainty avoidance low, and power distance low. Eastern cultures often tend to be more High Context, collectivism, uncertainty avoidance high, and power distance high. Both tools will give you a good idea of what to expect from them, and how to behave toward groups from other countries.

However, these are just a guideline. We are all uniquely different. Remember the Culture of One we learned earlier? You can't judge a book by its cover. Additionally, each country's positions on these dimensions are relative, not absolute.

Let me explain.

We all have our typical tendencies, such as "I'm generally a Low Context person." But that doesn't become your label. But depending on who you are talking to in what situation, we could shift on the scale of these frameworks.

Let's say you consider yourself to be relatively Low Context, just like me, and you would normally communicate quite eloquently, directly, assertively, explicitly. But what if you are put into a room full of Hollywood stars and they surround you to have a conversation? You would most likely become less talkative, use bigger and more vague words, be less assertive, etc. You shift to more "High Context." Right?

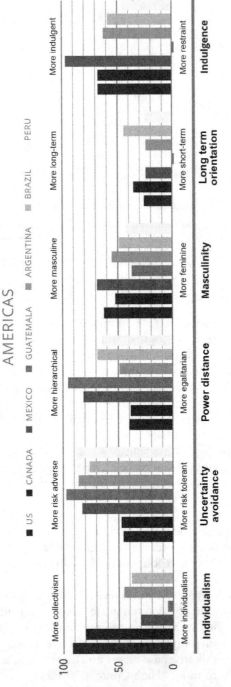

Hofstede's Cultural Dimensions comparison by countries in the Americas

Note: This figure compares the countries of Argentina, Brazil, Canada, Guatemala, Mexico, Peru, and US.

Source: Data from "Country Comparison Tool," The Culture Factor, accessed August 2023, https://www.hofstede-insights.com/country-comparison-tool. License for use granted by The Culture Factor Group – Hofstede Insights Oy.

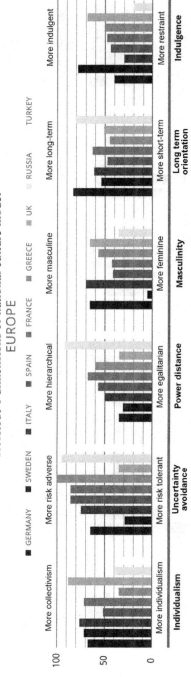

Hofstede's Cultural Dimensions comparison by countries in Europe

Note: This figure compares France, Germany, Greece, Italy, Russia, Spain, Sweden, Turkey, and United Kingdom.

Source: Data from "Country Comparison Tool," The Culture Factor, accessed August 2023, https://www.hofstede-insights.com/country-comparison-tool. License for use granted by The Culture Factor Group – Hofstede Insights Oy.

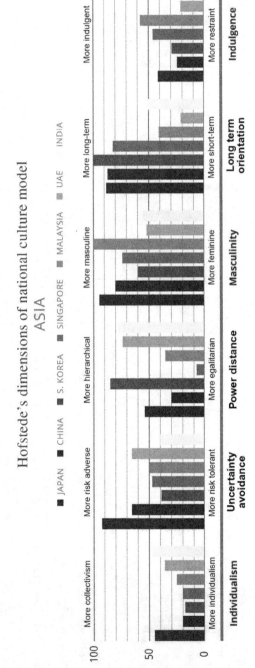

Hofstede's Cultural Dimensions comparison by countries in Asia

Note: This figure compares China, India, Japan, Malaysia, Singapore, South Korea, and United Arab Emirates.

Source: Data from "Country Comparison Tool," The Culture Factor, accessed August 2023, https://www.hofstede-insights.com/country-comparison-tool. License for use granted by The Culture Factor Group – Hofstede Insights Oy.

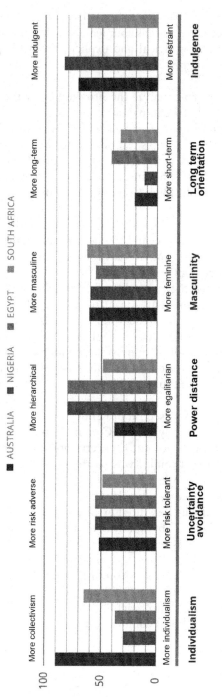

Hofstede's Cultural Dimensions comparison by countries in Oceania and Africa

Note: This figure compares Australia, Egypt, Nigeria, and South Africa.

Source: Data from "Country Comparison Tool," The Culture Factor, accessed August 2023, https://www.hofstede-insights.com/country-comparison-tool. License for use granted by The Culture Factor Group – Hofstede Insights Oy. As of October 2023 the scores and terminology was updated by The Culture Factor Group, the organization running www.hofstede-insights.com.

Let's think about another situation. You are as direct and explicit as you always are. But this new person joins your team, and he is even more direct – even blunt – and extremely logical and explicit. From his point of view, you'll be perceived as a higher context person.

It's all relative.

So it's important that you analyze the situation every time. Culture can be used meaningfully only by comparison.

With that said, High Context–Low Context and Dimensions of National Culture are still very effective tools to understand the "outer layer" of the Culture of One, and anticipate what you might expect from them.

Let's go back to Mr. Nakano and analyze what happened, using two effective cross-cultural tools, High Context–Low Context and Dimensions of National Culture.

Mr. Nakano comes from a "masculine" Japanese culture, was highly "collective" and "power distance high" – he expects loyalty to this group, and expects people around him to treat him with high respect. He was "uncertainty avoidance high" – that's why he hired a strategy consultant to make sure that his strategy would work, even though he was already quite experienced and confident. He also has the "long-term orientation" and views any shortcut as cheating. He heads a company that has been successfully conducting a traditional business for over 400 years, so the "restraint" orientation is quite strong. Finally, he kept using two words to communicate his intentions, and it is your job to understand what he really means without troubling him to spell everything out ("High Context").

What about me? I was focused on presenting *my* strategy ("individualistic") explicitly and assertively ("Low Context" and "masculine"), willing to take chances with a shortcut ("uncertainty avoidance – low" and "short-term orientation"). I think I was on the same page as Mr. Nakano in terms of the "restraint" index, but I believed my position was equal to Mr. Nakano's ("power distance – low").

Now you understand why I got fired by Mr. Nakano! As we say in Japanese, I "stepped on his face" by ignoring all the social relationships and telling everybody that he was wrong.

Your turn.

No, not to step on anyone's face! You just received two effective cross-cultural tools –High Context–Low Context, and Dimensions of National Culture. Let's put these tools into practice.

The analysis of cross-cultural communication gap comes in three steps.

Step 1: analyze them

First, think about a person you often experience conflict with. Someone you'd rather avoid talking to.

Do you have "that person" in mind?

Let's map out that person using two tools we just learned, High Context–Low Context and Dimensions of National Culture. Observe their behavioral and communication tendencies.

Are they more "explicit" or "implicit"?

Are they more "I-Focused" or "We-Focused"?

Are they more "risk tolerant" or "risk averse"?

Are they more "egalitarian" or "hierarchical"?

Are they more "masculine" or "feminine"?

Are they more "short-term oriented" or "long-term oriented"?

Are they more "indulgent" or "repressed"?

Refer to Figure on page 31 and mark on each scale where this person is. Remember to take into consideration how extreme each tendency is, as no one is perfectly middle and balanced.

LOW Context   **HIGH Context**
Explicit   Implicit

Individualism   **Collectivism**
"I" focused   "We" focused

LOW Uncertainty avoidance   Uncertainty avoidence HIGH
Risk tolerant   Risk averse

LOW Power distance   **Power distance HIGH**
Egalitarian   Hierarchical

Masculine   **Feminine**
Power important   Nurture & harmony important

Short-Term orientation   **Long-Term orientation**
Immediate result   Futuristic

Indulgence   **Restraint**
Satisfaction is good   Normative repression

Illustration of High Context–Low Context model and Hofstede's Cultural Dimensions model

Step 2: analyze yourself

Now, repeat the process. But this time, analyze yourself.

What are your typical tendencies? Again, refer back to Figure and mark where you are on the cross-cultural scale.

Both you and the other person may shift on the scale, depending on who is around, what the situation is, or what your mood is like at that time. Think about the specific time when you had a conflict with this person, and map out the tendencies of that moment.

Step 3: observe the gap

Now, observe the gap. Where are you in relation to where "that person" is?

When you compare yourself and others using the same scale, you can gauge where the gap is and how big. This will help you to gain great insights into what caused the miscommunication, misunderstanding, or mistrust between you and your global counterpart.

Let's think about what might be expected to happen between two different cultures.

Since I'm Japanese, living in the United States, let me continue to use the U.S.–Japan comparison.

Consider a scenario involving a global business opportunity for a company whose headquarters are based in Japan, a culture considered extremely High Context, relatively collective and power distance large, extremely uncertainty avoidance high, masculine, long-term–oriented, and somewhat restrained. The company decides to expand its operations to the United States, a culture considered relatively Low Context, highly individualistic, uncertainty avoidance and power distance are relatively low, slightly more masculine, very short-term–oriented, and relatively indulgent.

Analyze the communication gap using the High Context–Low Context model, as well as Hofstede's Dimensions of National Culture, as you read along the following case study.

U.S.–Japan Case Study

One of the top Japanese technology companies, ZenMaster Corp., headquartered in Kyoto, is known for its cutting-edge technology. It decided to expand its operations to the United States. It recently developed an innovative AI-based product and was eager to penetrate the American market. The American counterpart, fast-growing TechMatrix Corp., was excited about the partnership, as it promised lucrative opportunities.

They have been meeting virtually over the past few years to discuss the potential collaboration, and it's time to finalize the deal. ZenMaster's chief engineer, Yoshio Suzuki, and his team flew to the United States to meet with TechMatrix' executive team.

The meeting is held at TechMatrix's headquarters in Mountain View, California.

TechMatrix's president, John Smith, approaches Mr. Suzuki with wide open arms.

"Yoshio! Hi! So great to finally meet you in person! Wow, you are taller than I thought!!" John gives Mr. Suzuki a big welcoming hug.

Mr. Suzuki and his team look a bit stunned, but Mr. Suzuki awkwardly shakes John's hand.

"Oh . . . haha, OK . . . It is my great pleasure to meet you as well, Mr. John."

John continued, "You know, you can't really tell what you *really* look like over the Zoom screen! You know what I mean? I may be wearing no underwear and you don't even know. Hahaha!!"

His big laughter echoes in the hallway, and his sidekick and the vice president of TechMatrix, Nicole laughs along with John and says, "I knew it, John!! I'm always properly dressed on Zoom!! In my yoga pants!!"

TechMatrix team members all love John for always being so approachable, open, and humorous.

John turns to a man standing next to Mr. Suzuki.

"And you are . . . ?"

"Oh, I apologize for not introducing myself sooner. I am ZenMaster Corp.'s engineer department Unit 1 technician, Matsumoto Ken. Nice to meet you."

Ken hands his business cards.

"Nice to meet you too, Matsu . . . ah, Ken, Ken, right?"

"Yoshio and Ken, this is our famous meeting room. Would you like some coffee? Tea? Soda? Orange juice? Lemonade? Energy drink? Kombucha? You name it! Help yourself right there."

John points to an extensive drink bar in the "meeting room," or a lounge with bright colored sofas and modern designed asymmetric coffee tables all around the room. On the wall is a floor-to-ceiling covered ivy trimming the company logo. This is where his team members gather to take a break, do brainstorming, have an open discussion, or just to hang out.

"Oh, OK. Ahm, great."

Mr. Suzuki is the first to head to the drink bar. One of his team members, Ken, rushes to catch up with him and asks, "Chief, what would you like? Tea? OK, sir. Please."

Ken gestures to encourage Mr. Suzuki to have a seat and wait.

After a brief introduction by John, the meeting starts with Mr. Suzuki's remarks.

"Thank you so much for this opportunity to meet with us today. We have been discussing the collaboration opportunity for the past few years, and we are thrilled to finally be here. We may be a large company in Japan, but a no-name company in the world. We appreciate your trust in us. We have prepared the best solution for you. Ken will explain."

Ken starts presenting. First, ZenMaster's history, followed by philosophy and values, and the company's track record with some case studies. At the end of his 15-minute presentation, he briefly touches on the product's features.

John's team members interject with questions as Ken goes over the features. Ken seems a bit uncomfortable getting disrupted during the presentation. Nonetheless, John's team keeps asking questions, including John saying, "Why would the implementation phase take as long as four months? That's too long. We need one month. At the longest, 1½ months. What can you do about it? If we need some assistance in this phase, who's in charge?"

Ken explains, "We all have to work together toward the maximum result. To make sure that there is no unexpected consequences, we need to follow the protocol and test the system one step at a time. We don't want to launch the service until everything is tested and perfected."

Ken turns to Mr. Suzuki for confirmation. With Mr. Suzuki's nodding, Ken continues.

"Our team can assist you with marketing, as well. Our past clients' success is largely due to our grass-roots marketing activity."

Nicole proposes a new idea.

"Well, I'm thinking we need to build a quick awareness among our early adapters, so TikTok and some other social media would be the way to go. I can create video contents fairly quickly and frequently. What do you think?"

Mr. Suzuki then takes over and says, "Ms. Nicole, our grass-roots marketing has been working well, and it works well with the type of system we develop. It needs side-by-side guidance and relationship building with clients, so that we are always there to assist our clients."

Nicole interjects, "I understand. But TechMatrix's clients don't fit the mold. In my opinion, we need a different marketing strategy."

John adds on.

"I agree and disagree with Nicole. Yes, I agree that we need a different marketing strategy, but I feel that we need something more robust than social media."

Mr. Suzuki concludes the presentation by saying, "We'd like to build a long-term relationship with your team. Success doesn't happen overnight. We would like to ask for your utmost support in making this partnership successful together."

John and his team seem unsatisfied. Their questions are not directly answered yet.

John suggests that they take a 15-minute break and come back to a "deep dive" discussion.

Mr. Suzuki and his team seem perplexed. Despite John's encouragement to step out and breath the air in Mountain View and take a sip of coffee,

Mr. Suzuki's team gathers in one place and starts an impromptu team meeting in Japanese.

Hall's High Context–Low Context

Now, what cultural gaps have you identified? Using two cross-cultural models, let's decode this case.

Japan being a High Context culture values subtlety, reading between the lines, and relying on implicit understanding. On the other hand, United States is a Low Context culture, where direct communication and explicit information are crucial for effective communication.

John's team kept asking detailed, to-the-point questions for clarification. They also wanted a "deep dive" discussion to sit down and talk it out. For John's team being in a Low Context culture, meetings are a place to discuss openly, surface underlined issues, and bring out ideas to problem-solve. Furthermore, voicing one's disagreement, like John did with Nicole, is a token of contribution to a meaningful discussion. "I like you, but I don't like your opinion" is accepted, and even respected.

For a High Context culture like Mr. Suzuki's team, meetings are a place to confirm consensus and build harmony within a team. Surfacing disagreement during the meeting disturbs the harmony, and in such case, a separate smaller internal meeting should be held to mitigate those issues before conducting an official meeting again.

Hofstede's Dimensions of National Culture

Individualism vs. collectivism

Mr. Suzuki's team emphasized the collective effort and teamwork behind the product's development. They spoke in terms of "we" and "our team." On the other hand, the TechMatrix team tended to highlight personal contributions to projects. They spoke in terms of "I" and "my opinion."

This tendency shows up even in how they introduced themselves.

Ken comes from a collectivism culture where group comes first. He introduced himself as "ZenMaster Corp.'s engineer department Unit 1 technician, Matsumoto Ken."

In this order, he shared: the company he works for, a group he belongs to, his title there, his family name, then his first name. Group first, individual last.

And yet, John went straight to call Ken and Mr. Suzuki by their first names. Individual first.

When ZenMaster's team referred to their collective effort, TechMatrix's executives assumed they were being evasive or perhaps even trying to hide individual shortcomings. This led to doubts about the team's expertise and commitment to the project.

Uncertainty avoidance

Japan, with a high uncertainty avoidance culture, prefers to follow well-established protocols and minimize risks. In contrast, the United States has a more relaxed approach to risk and uncertainty.

ZenMaster's implementation protocol involves a step-by-step testing process to ensure that they can avoid any uncertain consequences. On the other hand, TechMatrix wanted to implement quickly, and if something happens, they'll fix it as they move forward.

Additionally, TechMatrix's executives proposed exploring new markets and unconventional marketing strategies for the product's launch. However, ZenMaster's team was hesitant and preferred sticking to traditional approaches, leading to misunderstandings about their willingness to adapt to new ideas.

Power distance

Mr. Suzuki was highly respected in ZenMaster, and his decisions were rarely questioned. He had a commanding presence and expected deference from his team members. In contrast, TechMatrix had a flatter hierarchy, whereby executives were more approachable and ideas were openly debated.

During the meeting, Mr. Suzuki's team presented the product's features briefly, assuming that their American counterparts would pick up on the underlying message. They felt it unnecessary to elaborate on technical details, thinking it might be perceived as condescending.

However, TechMatrix's executives expected more in-depth information, including technical specifications, data sheets, and market analysis. They felt that the presentation lacked substance and was too ambiguous.

Furthermore, in a power distance high culture like Japan, the highest ranked person never has to go get his own coffee! Remember how Ken ran to get a drink for Mr. Suzuki?

Masculinity vs. femininity

Both ZenMaster and TechMatrix are from cultures with relatively high masculinity, valuing assertiveness and achievement.

During the discussion about the marketing approach, both sides were assertive and competitive in their positions, resulting in a deadlock. Each party pushed its own ideas, and neither was willing to compromise, as it might be perceived as a sign of weakness.

Long-term orientation

ZenMaster had a long-term orientation, focusing on long-term relation-ship, gradual growth and long-range planning. TechMatrix's was more result-oriented, emphasizing quick returns on investments.

When TechMatrix proposed a short-term marketing campaign to quickly capture market attention, ZenMaster's team might have misunder-stood their intentions, assuming they lacked a commitment to the product's long-term success.

Indulgence vs. restraint

Japan's culture of restraint emphasizes modesty and humility in public interactions. In contrast, the American culture of indulgence encourages self-expression and enthusiasm.

During the 15-minute break, the ZenMaster team displayed restraint by not stretching their legs. They had only 15 minutes to regroup. They'd rather spend the time to discuss a strategy. However, TechMatrix's team might have perceived this as uptight, creating a rift between the teams.

* * *

Your turn.

Can you think of a potential scenario in your cross-cultural situation? If you are curious to learn what the research says about each country's tendency, I highly recommend going to Hofstede Insights (www.hofstede-insights.com/country-comparison-tool) and play with different countries.

But again, I can't stress more that these tools are only guidelines. Always remember the Culture of One. You want to be curious about what the gap is and where it comes from with someone facing right in front of you. Cre-ating the culturally inclusive environment and trusting relationship starts at the individual level. Let's close the gap one person at a time.

* * *

We have learned how to Acknowledge.

We have learned how to Analyze.

Now, we are going to learn the third A: Adapt.

When you identify a communication gap, how do you Adapt, so you can understand them and be understood, regardless of culture or value differences?!

Depending on the situation, your strategy could be very different.

We will explore three different scenarios: 1) when presenting to a global audience, 2) when managing a global team, and 3) when talking one-on-one.

But first and foremost, there are three important rules of thumb that you want to remember regardless of the situation. Are you ready?

Notes

1 Edward T. Hall, *Beyond Culture* (New York: Anchor Books, 1977), 14, 69, 127.

- SOPTV ED and Robert Harrison, "Iceberg Concept Images and PDF's," PBS LearningMedia, accessed April 3, 2024, infographic, https://indiana. pbslearningmedia.org/resource/a353a4ba-cd56-4999-97dd-0e40e11a7211/ iceberg-concept-of-culture-images-and-pdfs/.

2 Hall, *Beyond Culture*, 44–45, 57–69, 127, 160–161.
3 Hall, *Beyond Culture*, 44–45.
4 Hall, *Beyond Culture*, 63, 66.
5 Hall, Beyond Culture, 63.
6 Hall, Beyond Culture, 66.
7 Geert Hofstede, *Culture's Consequences: Comparing Values, Behaviors, Institutions and Organizations Across Nations*, 2nd ed. (Thousand Oaks: Sage Publications, 2003), 29.

Chapter 2

Focus on One BIG Message®

When you are talking to a culturally diverse group of people, your message has to be crystal clear.

Unlike recording a video, which you can rewind and replay again and again until you get the message right, when you speak live, you only get one shot.

How do you most effectively Adapt, so your message is not only clearly heard, but also acted upon?

Here are a few scenarios in which you may need to communicate:

1. It's a one-time gig.
2. You give the same presentation to multiple different groups of people. Different groups of people have different interests, focus, value system. One group could be salespeople, another research and development (R&D) engineers, another accountants. Different group, different values. So even if you are delivering the same message, *how* you verbalize it would be slightly different. (Also, I explore more in Chapter 3 about Main Points, but if you are delivering the same One BIG Message to different groups of people, supporting information [a.k.a. Main Points] would be different.)
3. You give different presentations to the same group of people over some period of time.

This chapter will be geared more toward single presentations (rather than a series of presentations). However, even if you are delivering a series of talks or presentations, your One BIG Message will need to adapt based on the micro goal of each session each time.

Taking my presentation training as an example, I often give three or four training sessions to the same group of people, and each session has a different agenda. But my overall goal is to equip them with effective global presentation skills, and "the importance of You-Focused One BIG Message" is emphasized in every single session.

DOI: 10.4324/9781003455615-3

Let's go through three rules of thumb that are important for you to remember, whether you are presenting to a global audience, managing a global team, or talking one-on-one.

Rule 1: the rule of KISS

The first tool to Adapt effectively is the rule of KISS.

Have you ever heard a speaker who uses very high-level language?

Have you given a speech that was at the wrong level for your audience, or have you used too much jargon?

I have been guilty of that, too.

Right after I finished my MBA program, I used all the "intelligent" terminologies I had learned in my management class. I wanted to sound like a "MBA graduate" and a "top consultant."

Many speakers make the same mistake I made, thinking that using high-level language makes us look intelligent.

Quite the contrary.

You must choose your words carefully to build credibility and sound intelligent, *However*, most importantly, you want your message to be understood by every single audience member!

Especially when you are speaking to the global audience, it's crucial to simplify your language that is *also* specific so that your message is crystal clear, leaving no room for inferences. Remember High Context–Low Context? If your use of language is more High Context, which means vague and indirect, you leave a huge room for inferences. This results in misunderstanding, miscommunication, and mistrust.

The more experience you have in your industry, and the deeper your knowledge, means that jargon can become your standard language.

But when you remove the jargon, you have the power to make your message stick.

Don't get me wrong. I recognize that jargon can be useful at times.

With jargon, communication can become more efficient and you may be able to convey precise technical meanings quickly. But unless you are presenting to an exclusive group of people who share the same exact knowledge, it can be off-putting, and will throw up barriers against "outsiders."

Your job as a speaker, is to *not* sound like the Shakespeare of your industry, but to get down to the audience's eye level and speak their language.

To be honest with you, Simple language is much harder to use than jargon.

So what do we do?

Always keep the rule of KISS in your mind.

KISS, usually stands for "Keep It Simple and Short" or "Keep It Simple, Stupid."

But I take it one step further:

Keep
It
Simple
Specific

Let me explain simply and specifically!

A highly educated and intelligent information technology (IT) engineer was preparing to speak at a board meeting. In our coaching session, this is what he originally had in his script:

> The new WoW is going to work great. But the thing is, it's actually not really new. It has been our consistent approach to manage a new project, helping our team to invest our time into building products to meet the real needs of people, and at the same time, reduce the risks of tons of work on initial phase of projects that will never go live or get approved, and also sidestep the need for huge amounts of initial project funding with expensive product launches or failures.

Do you understand this?

You are reading this in writing now, so you can re-read as many times as necessary until you understand it. It's still hard to understand!!

But when this message is verbally communicated, your audience can't replay you!! What if your audience is distracted by something and missed what you said? What if your audience is a global audience? The hurdle is even higher.

When you have a series of run-on sentences like this example, it sounds way too complicated. On top of that, he started with jargon. You will lose your audience this way for sure.

When I asked him what "WoW" meant, he said "oh . . . it means way of working," as if he wanted to say, "of course you should know that!" But it turned out that this terminology was used only within his team!

He also used some vague language, like "great," "thing," "tons," "people," "huge."

How can you rephrase this more simply and specifically?

First of all, don't assume your listener knows jargon or acronyms, especially culturally diverse audiences. Removing jargon ensures that your message remains accessible and easily comprehensible to all listeners. Remember, in a cross-cultural situation, your common sense may not be so common.

Second, break up a paragraph into shorter sentences. It's difficult for any audience to catch everything in a long sentence. Moreover, when you break up into shorter sentences, your speech becomes more rhythmical. In oral communication, information presented with a rhythmic cadence is easier to remember and recall.

Third, keep asking yourself, "what do I really mean?"; "How can I say it differently, so my word choice adds the most value?"; "So what?"

What on earth is "WoW"?

What is "the thing?"

How much is "tons" and huge"?

What do you really mean? How can you say it differently, so your word choice adds value?

Choosing the word simply and specifically would also help reduce "room for inferences," so your culturally diverse audience will understand exactly what you mean.

What if he rewrote his script like this?

Until today, nearly half of our product development projects never came to fruition.

The new way of working I'm proposing will change this.

First, we will be able to invest our time to build only products that are truly needed in the market.

As a result, we can reduce the risk of project failure.

This means that each project will produce an improved return on investment.

Can you see the difference with clear, concise communication?

It's Simple and Specific. Right?

Instead of words like "thing," "tons," or "stuff," select the most appropriate, Specific language. Never be vague. Use exact, precise words with power and value. Using more Specific language builds your credibility and adds merit to what you are saying.

Otherwise, you'll lose your audience when they hear vague, weak, or overused words.

What Simple and Specific words can you replace with "thing"? How many Specific words can you come up with?

Think about these alternative words, carry them with you, and use them to add precision and power to your presentations and conversations.

Another example.

In 2016, former U.S. First Lady Michelle Obama's speech went viral for her take on what it means to be the bigger person in the face of hate: "When they go low, we go high." This phrase made news headlines all over the world and has even been plastered onto T-shirts.

At the Democratic National Convention in 2020, Michelle used the same phrase again, and reminded viewers of the need to take the high road, despite the unprecedented challenges that 2020 brought.

> Going high is the only thing that works, because when we go low – when we use those same tactics of degrading and dehumanizing others – we just become part of the ugly noise that's drowning out everything else. We degrade ourselves. We degrade the very causes for which we fight.[1]

For a message to be memorable, you need to use Simple language that everyone would understand – no matter what culture they are from. The language has to bring clarity into the picture, so everyone who hears the message will be able to paint a clear image. It may be a clear vision of their future, the actions they need to take, or to imagine the concept of the products/services/ideas the speaker is presenting.

Michelle did just that.

She effectively anchored a message by making it both: 1) KISS, and 2) fewer than ten words – "When they go low, we go high." Just seven words. Superb line.

If the message is too long, people are unlikely to remember or recall.

Tune in to the rule of KISS, or your audience will tune out.

Rule 2: focus on your One BIG Message

The second – and I would say the most important – rule you need to remember when communicating your idea is to focus on what I call One BIG Message.

"When they go low, we go high" was Michelle Obama's One BIG Message.

One BIG Message is the high-level message that you want your audience to take away and remember well. It has to be consistent throughout your communication and logically tied to any piece of information you provide to support your One BIG Message.

But that doesn't mean that you have to provide a long list of information to support your idea. Quite the contrary. The more you give away, the less clarity your listeners will receive.

It's so easy as leaders and experts in our field to want to give too much away when we communicate.

I used to think that a great speaker was a content-rich speaker.

But too much content will only confuse people, especially if you are speaking to a culturally diverse audience – they may need more time to digest your messages.

Imagine that as soon as you start writing something down, the speaker goes on to say something else worth noting and you can't catch it.

In fact, I once had an opportunity to sit on the front row at a professional speakers convention. One of the keynote speakers was a very well-respected, hall of fame speaker who has appeared on national TV many times. His energy, his dynamic delivery, and how he kept the audience on the edge of their seats were all so amazing! I was on the front row, and he kept coming to me and grabbing my shoulder . . . as if he was hypnotizing me or anointing me.

In his 60-minute keynote, he gave 50 important points he wanted us to write down.

50! That's almost one every minute!

At first, every time he said "write this down!," I tried my best to write them down in my notebook. I couldn't catch up. My hand started to hurt, so I took out my laptop, because I type much faster than handwrite. I still couldn't catch up. And trust me when I say that I type fast. I mean, FAST! I even won a typing competition back in high school.

But while I was typing down all of his important messages, he would move on to the next point before I was halfway through. Everything he said was so important, I ended up typing nothing, and remembered nothing.

All I remember was his energy. Maybe I *was* being hypnotized the entire time!

But here is one big thing I learned from him.

When you say everything, you say nothing.

When we start to learn more and more about our topic, that "more" ends up finding its way into our communication.

What's important to realize about effective cross-cultural communications is that *less is more*.

Just because you know more doesn't mean you have to show more all at once. Even if your listeners are not culturally diverse, information overload will not help them understand the most important point you are trying to make.

And this is one of the biggest pitfalls that many speakers and leaders fall into. Even experienced speakers.

You may have so many ideas pulling you in different directions, and it's easy to get lost when it comes to persuasive communication.

By distilling your thoughts into One BIG Message, you can communicate your message with power and persuasion. Just like Michelle Obama did with her One BIG Message: "When they go low, we go high." Simple. Specific. Succinct.

Now, what exactly is One BIG Message?

Think of it like an umbrella.

Concept of One BIG Message

First, you need a fabric to cover yourself, right?

The fabric is the design of your choice.

That's the first and, maybe, the only thing that people will see. And you want them to notice it!! Of course, there have to be solid frames to hold up the umbrella, but that's not the first thing you want them to pay attention to. (Unless you are a product engineer!) The fabric is the canvas of your message, story, statement, style, etc., and you want it to stick out. Memorable.

That's your One BIG Message.

You can include other details as necessary, but only to support your One BIG Message, but not so much that it distracts from the most important message that you want to convey.

In order to have persuasive communication in any situation, but especially in a cross-cultural situation, you must find your One BIG Message, so that there is no ambiguity or room for multiple interpretations left.

As previously mentioned, when you want to communicate effectively, especially in a cross-cultural situation, *less* is *more*.

What is *one thing* that you want your audience to remember – and remember well? Can you say it simply and specifically ("Rule of KISS"), and in fewer than ten words? Can you think of different ways to say it until your message is rhythmical and memorable, so that it can be recalled and repeated over and over?

That's your One BIG Message.

But choosing your One BIG Message is challenging! In fact, it's the hardest part of developing a speech or presentation or any communication.

Have you ever listened to a speech or presentation and thought:

"What's the point she's trying to make?"
"How did he come to that conclusion?"
"That's interesting, but I'm fine with my same old way"

In all of these cases, the speaker probably suffered from poor "Logos."

Logos is a Greek word which derives from the English word logic.

The Greek philosopher Aristotle said that in order for people to feel fully persuaded, you need to have the following three elements in your communication.

- Logos: appealing to logic
- Pathos: appealing to emotions
- Ethos: appealing to ethics, morals, and character.[2]

Persuasion Triad

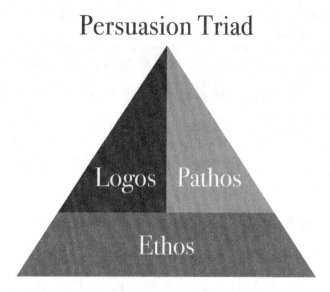

Concept of the Persuasion Triad: Logos, Pathos, Ethos

This is called the Persuasion Triad. If you are lacking any of these elements, your persuasive power will greatly diminish. However, since we are talking about logic here, let's focus on "Logos."

At this point, some of you may be thinking, "what's Logos to do with One BIG Message? It doesn't flow logically!"

It actually has a great deal to do with One BIG Message.

Without a logical thinking foundation, it's almost impossible to develop a clear, compelling, and memorable One BIG Message.

Why?

Because you have so much valuable information and insights you want to convey, but you need to focus on one – yes, just one – message that summarizes them all. You need the skill to organize, sort out, and prioritize pieces of information. In order to do that, you need a strong foundation of logical thinking approach.

Before guiding you through using logical thinking to create your One BIG Message, let's discuss why you need "logic," and what "logic" or "logical" means.

Logic, by definition, is "the study of correct reasoning, especially regarding making inferences."[3]

If your communication is hard to follow, or if your argument or reasoning is not strong enough, your listeners will easily dismiss your ideas.

Sound, logical arguments, on the other hand, are hard for your audience to ignore.

For example, I could tell you that:

"This is the best iPhone to use because it has a long battery life."

For your listener, however, the best phone may be another model with better camera. Or it could be the one with better connectivity.

With this argument, I'm leaving out "You-Focused" perspectives – their point of view. As a result, my argument sounds not persuasive enough for them.

Also, we want to be careful about using absolute terms, like "best," "only," "everyone," "perfect." People's perceptions are different, so absolute terms could also compromise logic.

What if I improved my argument and said:

"When you're dashing from meeting to meeting and always on the go, you need an iPhone that has a long battery life so you don't lose connection with the people that matter the most."

Do you see the difference?

I've related my facts to my audience because I know they are busy people who don't have time to charge their phones several times in a day.

I've set up a situation that they can relate to, and now they're interested in what I have to say.

The key here is to have a clear understanding of your audience, because without that, you will lack the connection to the logic.

I call it "You-Focused" as opposed to "I-Focused."

If you are still thinking,

"But logic is dry and cold and boring,"
"Logic doesn't help me become an entertaining and fun speaker," or
"You can't build emotional connection just using logic,"

you are not wrong there. You may be actually right, *if* only Logos in the Persuasion Triad is overemphasized. As mentioned before, you need all three elements in good balance; otherwise, it causes: "She is absolutely right! But . . . I'm not quite feeling it . . . ."

But that does NOT mean that Logos can be taken less seriously.

In fact, it is extremely important to structure your communication, craft your message, and get your audience's buy-in, especially for those who tend to put more emphasis on Pathos, or the emotional factor.

Here is why.

The preconceptions of your listeners will not easily be pushed aside.

If your communication is hard to follow, or if your arguments are fairly weak, your listeners will find it easy to dismiss your ideas.

Sound, logical arguments, on the other hand, are hard for your listeners to ignore.

Once again, I can't emphasize enough that we need a good balance of Logos, Pathos, and Ethos. However, if you lack one aspect of the Persuasion Triad, you will lose your listeners.

When combined with good Ethos and Pathos, strong Logos will mean all but the most stubborn listeners to give strong consideration to your ideas.

Typical patterns of flaws in logic

Let's now think about what causes your communication to be less logical or persuasive.

Here is an example.

Let's say I want to convince you to try my diet approach. It's called "the cake diet."

If you know me personally, you know, that I'm the cake queen. I. *Love*. Cakes! I'm always thinking about how I can have a cake and eat it, too!!

In fact, let's say my One BIG Message is: "You can have a cake and eat it, too!"

Here is my argument:

If you LOVE cakes like I do, but you also want to lose weight, you don't need to give up on cakes anymore! My cake diet allows you to have a cake and eat it, too! In my personal experience, I've gained weight from the stress of *not* eating cakes. You know stress is the enemy of weight loss! The other day, when I ate a cake, however, I lost weight the next day! So the cake diet works! I can even recommend where to get the best cake! It's $40 a slice in Tokyo, Japan, but it's worth it! It's the world's best-tasting cake!!

What are you thinking in your head? Maybe something like this:

"Sugar is bad for you. Everyone knows that!"
"Maybe you had different kinds of stress that contributed to the weight gain."
"It was just a coincidence that you lost weight after eating a cake."
"Every diet that sounds too good to be true has failed in the past."
"This cake diet will fail miserably."

My One BIG Message – that "You can have a cake and eat it too!" – itself may be a clear, succinct, Simple, and Specific big idea. However, other pieces of information I communicated above don't support this One BIG Message in a logical manner.

Your audience will have had their own past exposure to situations, and will often have experienced a level of emotion with something like a failed diet. This means they would look to your arguments for flaws and reach a conflicting conclusion, so you need strong Logos to counter these preconceptions and conflicting conclusions.

If you listen to my argument again, you will find a leap in the logical flow. I also go off-track.

My logic was this.

The other day I ate a cake, and I lost weight. Therefore, the cake diet works.

Really?

Maybe I didn't eat anything else that day!

This cause and effect might be just a coincidence. Yet, I came to a firm conclusion that the cake diet works without enough evidence. Incomplete thinking.

Do you see a leap between my reasoning and conclusion?

What about my last statement – "I can recommend where to get the best cake! It's $40 a slice in Tokyo, Japan, but it's worth it. It's the world's best-tasting cake!!"?

Are we talking about the best-tasting cake here? Aren't we talking about how effective my cake diet is?

I just got excited talking about cakes, and recommended my favorite cake. But that's nothing to do with how a cake diet works. A $40 cake is a distraction from the argument with some sentiment that seems to be relevant but isn't really on-topic.

You can see that I went off-track.

(By the way, this $40 per slice cake is real. It's one of my most favorite cakes in Tokyo. You can reach me out privately to ask me about that cake! But when you do, please be easy on me for getting too excited and off-track!)

Back to logic.

My original statement takes a leap and goes off-track. In other words, the Logos is weak.

But what if I improve my argument like this?

"If you are a cake lover like I am, my cake diet allows you to *have a cake and eat it, too*" (seven-word One BIG Message)!

According to the research by "the diet institute," the three most important factors for successful weight loss are food, time, and exercise.

First, this cake is made of a special blend of active ingredients that accelerate weight loss. They are all natural, and if I didn't tell you, you wouldn't even know it was a diet cake.

Second, the timing is important. The best time of the day to consume this cake is mid-morning. Weight loss ingredients are activated while you move, and they are slowly released into your body over an 8-hour period.

Third, you need to stick with a recommended workout schedule. This workout program is specifically designed to activate the special ingredients.

I strictly followed these three factors for three months. Let me show you my before picture and after picture. You can see this cake diet is not only scientifically researched, but actually works. I'm the living proof.

Now you want to learn more about this cake diet, don't you?

That's the power of Logos. My One BIG Message is logically supported by my supporting statements.

But if you are not paying close attention, it's extremely easy to compromise on your Logos.

My foundation of persuasive communication skills was honed while I was working as a consultant at McKinsey & Company.

Before we go even deeper into persuasive communication, let me first share with you what I learned at McKinsey and how you can apply the concept into presentations, so you can communicate your idea with persuasively and powerfully.

Where is the "So What?"

When I was interning at McKinsey, I was assigned a research portion of a client project. I spent a full week working 15 hours a day to gather information, analyze it, and put it into a research report. I was quite confident at what I was presenting, except for one tiny detail. That one tiny detail didn't affect my argument, though, so I decided that this report was ready to be presented in front of the client.

A couple of days before our client meeting, my project manager and my mentor, Mr. Kawakubo, told me to present it to him first. *Good practice,*

I thought. Mr. Kawakubo was a mellow, gentle guy in his late 30s at that time. I was glad that he allowed me to practice my presentation with him first. After intensely listening to my 10 minutes of well researched, yet concise, presentation, Mr. Kawakubo gave me two words. Just two.

"So What?"

Shocked to hear this completely unexpected response, all I could do was to repeat back these two words.

". . . . So What . . . ?"

As an intern, I was still learning McKinsey terminology. I didn't know that this "So What?" question was one of the most important elements of their logical thinking technique.

Mr. Kawakubo continued, "McKinsey's clients are senior executives at large companies. These executives were smart, busy, and impatient, which means that they didn't want just the facts. They brought in McKinsey to provide analysis and insights, not to summarize. If we want to be a trusted, insightful adviser to CEOs and senior executives, we need to synthesize, not summarize. Anyone can summarize – synthesis is much more valuable. Synthesis = summary + insight."

This is when I first learned of the concept, "where is the 'So What?'" – and this has become the core principle for my persuasive communication crafting technique, Breakthrough Method®.

Just when I was about to leave the meeting room that day, Mr. Kawakubo stopped me and said one more thing.

"By the way, look further into this," he said, pointing exactly at that one tiny detail that I was certain nobody would notice. Only McKinsey consultants.

Since then, I developed the Breakthrough Method, which allows you to apply strategy consultants' logical thinking technique into speech and presentation crafting process.

Even though there are many elements that play big roles in crafting logically sound messages, I'm highlighting three foundational logical thinking concepts you need to know as a persuasive communicator – pyramid structure, MECE, and "So What?" "Why So?".

Pyramid structure

The pyramid principle is an approach originally invented by Barbara Minto and essential to the structured problem-solving approach I learned at McKinsey. Learning this approach has changed the way I look at any presentation since. Minto based her thinking around ideas ranging from Aristotle's persuasion triad and other sources on logic throughout history.

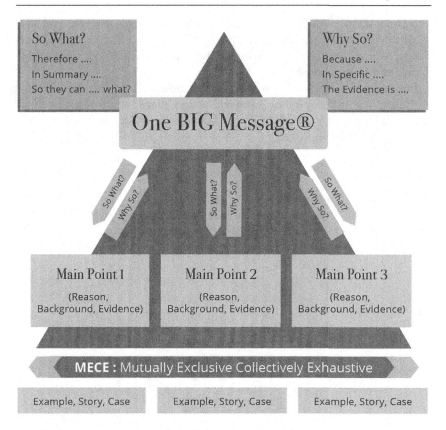

Pyramid structure, the foundation of logical thinking

The pyramid has three levels.

- Highest level: This is the overall takeaway from everything you have analyzed. It's a high-level message you want your audience to remember, and remember well. This is your One BIG Message. This One BIG Message has to be consistently emphasized and tied to any information you introduce throughout your presentation.
- Middle level: This level provides the synthesized arguments or takeaways of a group of arguments. This level serves as what I call "Main Points." These Main Points support One BIG Message. In Breakthrough Method, I teach global leaders to use The Power of Three – present three main points to support your One BIG Message. We often find things easier to follow when we can break it down into three key things. When you use The Power of Three, you can establish logic and simplicity,

making it easier for both you and the audience to stay on track. You can also provide balance and order, because there is a clear expectation of how you are progressing. This way, the audience will know where they are, and stay engaged.

- Lower level: This level provides information such as analysis, survey results, research, Specific examples, action plans, or stories that best describe each of your Main Point. This level provides more details for each of your Main Point.

MECE

You'll notice that it says "MECE" in the Figure below.

MECE is an acronym for the phrase Mutually Exclusive, Collectively Exhaustive. This means all points listed cover the entire range of ideas while also being unique and differentiated from each other without overlapping.

MECE

=

Mutually

Exclusive

Collectively

Exhaustive

Explanation of MECE

When you are presenting your idea, it's tempting to include a lot of (what you think are) important pieces of information. As a result, your message becomes complex and hard for your audience to follow.

MECE is the first logical thinking principle that will help you sharpen your thinking, sort out many different types and levels of information, and simplify complex ideas into something that can be easily understood and digested.

MECE is made up of two parts.

First, "mutually exclusive" is a concept from probability theory that says two events cannot occur at the same time. For example, if you flip a coin, you cannot get both heads and tails, as they are mutually exclusive.

When applied to information, mutually exclusive ideas would be distinctly separate and not overlapping.

Second, "collectively exhaustive" means that the set of ideas is inclusive of all possible options. Going back to the coin example, the set of "heads" and "tails" is mutually exclusive *and* collectively exhaustive.

Combining these two elements will allow you to take a large amount of information and simplify it into multiple groups of separate and distinct ideas.

Let me show you a Simple way to apply the concept of MECE.

Let's say you are doing a back-to-school shopping for your child, and here is a list of items to buy. Look at the list for 10 seconds.

1. Notebooks
2. Pencils
3. T-shirts
4. Lunch box
5. Socks
6. Jump ropes
7. Sneakers
8. Crayons
9. Erasers
10. Water bottle
11. Lunch bag
12. Pants

Now look away. Close your eyes. Try to remember as many of these items as possible.

How many did you remember? Not that easy, I suppose.

Using MECE as our guide, we take the list and try to create mutually exclusive groups. We might end up with the following 3 groups:

Group 1 – Stationaries: notebooks, pencils, crayons, erasers
Group 2 – Lunch items: lunch box, water bottle, lunch bag
Group 3 – Outfits: T-shirts, socks, sneakers, pants

Within the context of our list, the three groups we identified are distinctly different and separate. They are mutually exclusive. Additionally, our grouping covers all 12 items in the original list, so the grouping is "collectively exhaustive," as well.

In strategy consulting, consultants use MECE frequently when brainstorming ideas and breaking down a list of information into manageable groups; simplifying a long list of research data, facts, or information into a smaller set of ideas; creating an executive summary of a presentation; summarizing action items into a smaller number of high-level themes; breaking down a project into separate workstreams; designing a website or brochure and creating a menu of service offerings, etc.

As a persuasive communicator, you can use MECE to lay out your ideas in a pyramid structure so that you have one clear One BIG Message and three supporting points that are MECE.

We will revisit this pyramid structure in the next chapter. You will have an opportunity to build your own One BIG Message, as well as supporting Main Points.

Keep in mind that the MECE principle is not perfect – it is more of an ideal to push your logic in the right direction. Use it to continually improve and refine your story.

"So What?" "Why So?"

Remember Mr. Kawakubo, my mentor and project manager at McKinsey?

The "So What?" question is used by McKinsey consultants every day. When we delve into a solution of the problem, when we present anything to a client, always ask "So What?" at least five times. What is the implication of what we had found from our analysis? What is the data actually telling us? Why should our client care about what we have to say?

The concept was so fundamental to the work of strategy consultants that I regularly heard partners and project managers ask, "Where's the 'So What?'" as they reviewed a slide deck that was going to be presented to a client. As a intern, I was trained to think about what the key takeaway or implication was to the client, with each and every slide I created.

Equally important as "So What?" is "Why So?".

When you ask "So What?", you are digging deeper into the core issues. "Why So?" traces your thought process back to the higher level of information you started with.

For example, let's say you conducted interviews with 100 people in their 30s and asked if they were interested in switching jobs. You presented the result to recruiting agencies that 70 people said "yes."

Then, you ask yourself, "So What?"

What does this data mean for your clients? What action do you need to take?

At this point, you just presented a summary of the data you collected. But your job has just started. You need to provide synthesize. That's where you provide values.

If you say, "With this information, I can plan a career event targeted to people in their 30s," now you are synthesizing.

But you may say, "Where would this action lead them to?"

This is when you want to ask yourself: "Why So?"

Your answer to the "Why So?" will back up your synthesized statement. Why should a recruiting agency plan a career event targeted to people in their 30s? Why is this the right action?

If your answer to "Why So?" is something like:

Currently, your recruiting agency's core target is newly grads. However, the research shows that 70% of mid-career people in their 30s are interested in switching jobs. This means that this target segment most likely has a strong need to hire a recruiting agency. If your recruiting agency switches their core target from newly grads to mid-career candidates, and throws an event targeting mid-career candidates, your recruiting agency will very likely increase their business opportunity,

I am certain that your audience will be fully persuaded.

Asking "So What?" and "Why So?" helps you provide a sound, complete logic to accompany your statement.

Notice that you see "So What?" and "Why So?" in bilateral arrows in Figure on page 53.

"So What?" and "Why So?" strengthen your Logos, the logical connection between your One BIG Message and your supporting Main Points.

As we learned earlier, "So What?" and "Why So?" are two critical questions to craft your message strategically. The first question, "So What?", clarifies the logical connection between each of your Main Points and your One BIG Message.

Your Main Points are the facts, data, research findings, and statements that you use to back up your One BIG Message. These Main Points are the middle level of information in the pyramid structure, and all Main Points should be MECE.

Now, think about what is the implication of what we found in our research.

What is this Main Point actually telling us?

Why should they care?

Here are the Main Points. Therefore . . . What?

By asking "So What?" or "Why So?", they can . . . What?

You can check whether your Main Point logically explains your One BIG Message.

Look at the arrow pointing from Main Points to One BIG Message. Bottom Up.

You have Main Point 1. "So What?" One BIG Message.

You have Main Point 2. "So What?" One BIG Message.

You have Main Point 3. "So What?" One BIG Message.

"Why So?" Goes the other direction. From One BIG Message, to Main Points.

Your overall message is your One BIG Message.

Why did you come to such a conclusion?

In other words: "Why So?"

Check the logical connection again between One BIG Message and each Main Point, but this time, top-down.

Here is my One BIG Message. "Why So?" Because, Main Point 1.

Here is my One BIG Message. "Why So?" Because, Main Point 2.

Here is my One BIG Message. "Why So?" Because, Main Point 3.

Let's put it in practice.

Let's say, my One BIG Message is: "We can expect a market expansion with the acquisition of Company A."

I came to this conclusion from findings in my research and analysis.

First point is: "We will gain a competitive advantage from our combined human resources – we have a strong sales team, and Company A has a strong R&D team."

Second point is: "Company A's product portfolio complements ours, and we can expect product portfolio synergy."

Third point is: "Company A's corporate governance is diverse, and they utilize a female workforce."

Pyramid Structure, the foundation of logical thinking, case 1

Let's look at Main Point 1.

We'll gain competitive advantage from our combined human resources.

So What? What can you say from this Main Point?

"So we can expect market expansion from the acquisition of Company A."

"We can expect market expansion"

Why So? Why do you say that? What could possibly support your one big message?

Because we have a strong sales team, and Company A has a strong R&D team, meaning we'll gain competitive advantage.

Logically sound both ways. Right?

Main Point 2.

Company A's product portfolio complements ours, and we can expect product portfolio synergy"

So What?

"So we can expect market expansion from the acquisition of Company A."

"We can expect market expansion"

Why So?

Because there is a product portfolio synergy.

Logically sound, as well.

How about Main Point 3?

"Company A's corporate governance is diverse, and they utilize a female workforce."

So What?

"So we can expect market expansion from the acquisition of Company A."

"We can expect market expansion"

Why So?

Because corporate governance is diverse . . . . ?

What do you think?

That doesn't sound quite logical, does it?!

Diverse corporate governance doesn't necessarily contribute to market expansion.

One way to fix this logical disconnect is to update the Main Point 3.

But how?

Remember MECE.

How can you make Main Points 1, 2, and 3 to be Mutually Exclusive Collectively Exhaustive?

Because Main Point 1 is about People, and Main Point 2 is about Things. There is a well-known MECE framework called "People–Things–Money." Turning Main Point 3 into a money-related point is one way to keep all three main points MECE.

How about the following for Main Point 3?: "Company A's Scale of Economy would provide us cost advantage."

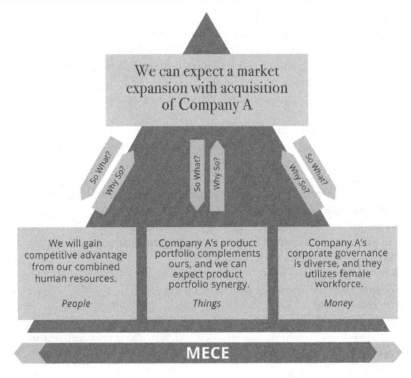

Pyramid Structure, the foundation of logical thinking, case 2

Or, if you wanted to highlight diversity, maybe your One BIG Message and Main Points should be adjusted to make your argument logically sound. In this case, your One BIG Message could be adjusted to something like: "We can reinforce our Diversity and Inclusion strategy with the acquisition of Company A" and Main Points to support this adjusted One BIG Message could highlight Company A's:

1. Corporate governance diversity
2. Workforce diversity
3. Supplier diversity

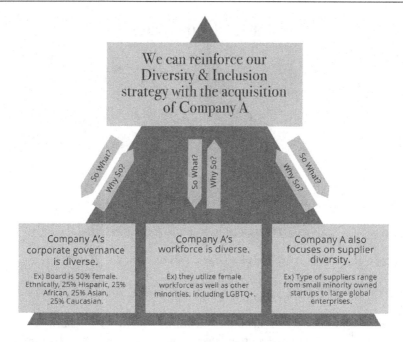

Pyramid Structure, the foundation of logical thinking, case 3

Only by asking "So What?" and "Why So?" in both directions between One BIG Message and each Main Point can you really check the logical flow.

When you are communicating with a culturally diverse audience, it is crucial that the clear One BIG Message is received by all, no matter what their value differences may be. In order to develop a persuasive message, you need a solid foundation of logical thinking skills. We will revisit this topic with more Specific business case, as well as your personal example, in the next chapter.

Rule 3: storytelling

Logical flow of your communication is quite important. However, Logos alone would not help you gain a buy-in from your diverse audience. You also need Ethos and Pathos.

Persuasion Triad

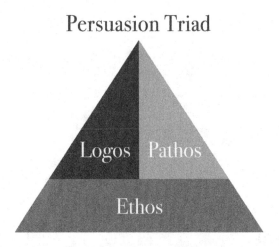

Concept of the Persuasion Triad – Logos, Pathos, Ethos

Ethos is a Greek word meaning "custom," "habit," or "character." It's one of the key elements of a great speech, including Logos and Pathos, and is essentially about establishing trust with your audience.

The great philosopher Aristotle said that people are more likely to believe someone who has convinced them of their good character. Moreover, he believed that we are more likely to be persuaded by someone who can be trusted, and is "similar to us."

That's key. In other words, if you can demonstrate to your audience that you are similar to them (in your values, interests, experience, struggles/frustrations, life stage, career stage, etc.), they will be more likely to trust you – and if the audience trusts you, then they will be more receptive to your ideas and expect that what you are telling them is true.

That is Ethos. If you have high Ethos, your audience will listen and pay attention from your first word.

Pathos is a Greek word meaning to "experience," "undergo," "suffer." It refers to the element in an experience that makes us feel compassion, pity, or sympathy.

Pathos is all about emotional impact. It's the ability to persuade by appealing to your audience's emotions.

Some of the most memorable and persuasive speeches I've heard have used lots of Pathos, stirring up incredible emotions that compelled me to change my thinking or take action. I would say that Pathos is the hardest – yet most powerful – thing to get right in persuasive speaking.

The most powerful way to achieve Pathos is by telling stories.

Identify which emotion(s) you want your audience to feel and the highlight areas of your speech that are going to draw on this emotion.

Show passion and emotion yourself in a way that feels natural to you. It doesn't need to be overly dramatic, but by genuinely feeling that emotion yourself, you will influence your audience, too.

Articulate your Why: This is your reason why anyone should care about what you have to say. Make it relevant and timely to the *here* and *now*.

Third effective way to Adapt is *not* just use complete logic, statistics, and data, but actually reach people's heart and connect emotionally. I call this technique "tell a story and make a point," also known as storytelling, because storytelling is a universal language.

If you haven't noticed, I've been telling you stories in this book already.

When you tell a story and make a point, your message makes impact at a deeper level.

You may remember Mr. Nakano, the chairman of the Japanese craft company from Chapter 1. In fact, Mr. Nakano told me his "No Shortcut" story. Because he used a story to make a point, I fully understood his values and visions, which were hidden in the part of the iceberg I couldn't see.

In business, we often focus too much on Logos and Ethos.

I have been emphasizing the importance of logic and logical thinking foundation. However, we humans are creatures of emotion. Logic alone will not persuade the other party completely. No matter how logically sound your message might be (Logos), or how respected your credentials might be (Ethos), Logos and Ethos alone will not invite them to take action.

Especially in a global business, your logic may not be their logic. Storytelling is the universal language, because stories touch human souls. Therefore, storytelling technique in a culturally diverse environment is highly effective to Adapt your message, and have your global audience take it to their heads, hearts, and minds.

You need Pathos.

For example, a scientist speaking at a world convention can talk about global warming and bring up facts and figures about how many tons of ice melt into the sea every year. There, she would be using Logos. However, by arguing about the impact of global warming on living things – for instance, how many polar bears will die if the current trend continues – she'll tap into the emotions of the audience. Pathos is the emotional vehicle that carries the Logos to the audience.

The same applies to communication within a business. For instance, say you are a department head presenting a quarterly performance review. You have to tell your team that their sales are down by 40% due to the pandemic and this trend will likely continue for the next few quarters. Instead of presenting the fact, you can start off by saying "This is a tough time.

I get it. And this is when we need to gather every bit of your creativity, so we can turn around the situation with our own hands."

In this business example, the Logos would be to show numbers, focus on goals and action plans, etc. Pathos would be to show empathy, and encourage and lift up their motivation.

Emotions are motivators, so the audience is more likely to be persuaded and act upon your message by using Pathos.

Pathos is more likely to increase the chances that your audience:

- Understands your point of view
- Agrees with your opinion
- Accepts your arguments
- Acts on your proposals
- Tells their friends about your message

If you have low Pathos, the audience is likely to try to find reasons to reject your proposals.

The single most effective way to strengthen Pathos is storytelling.

Great leaders, coaches, entrepreneurs, CEOs, authors, and speakers understand this. If there is one thing that they have in common, it is that they are great storytellers.

They understand that in order to influence people and move them to action, you have to be able to trigger their emotions – Pathos – and there is no better way to do that than to tell a compelling story.

Before you sell anything, you need your audience to connect with you. They need to understand your Why and identify with you on a more personal level.

The Why is your story.

But here is the thing. Very few leaders know how to articulate their Why, their reason for being and why anyone should even care. They don't have a formula to develop a story in a systematic way.

You may be a natural storyteller, but the ability to capture people's hearts through storytelling – and get them to listen, take action, buy from you or buy into you – requires skill, creativity, and strategy.

If you think you are not a natural storyteller, however, don't worry. You don't have to be a superhero to deliver powerful stories, but you do need the right tools and processes.

I have created the 6Cs of Strategic Storytelling™, that'll help you become more authentic, meaningful, and powerful by communicating your messages using storytelling, and you will learn this framework in the next chapter.

Let's put it all together. To make sure you achieve the right balance of Ethos, Logos, and Pathos, ask yourself: Does the audience respect you? Does your message evoke emotions? Does your One BIG Message make sense? If you can answer yes to all three questions, you're well on your way to persuading your audience.

Notes

1 Michelle Obama, "Michelle Obama's DNC speech," PBS NewsHour, August 17, 2020, YouTube video, 18:31, 8:53–9:14, https://www.youtube.com/watch?v=uKy3iiWjhVI.
2 Aristotle, Aristotle's *Art of Rhetoric*," trans. Robert C. Bartlett, 1st ed. (Chicago: University of Chicago Press, 2019).
3 Mica Giberti, "Logic – Is It Logical?", in *Rhetoric in Everyday Life*, ed. Alessandra Von Burg (Montreal: PressBooks, 2021), chap. 8, https://librarypartnerspress.pressbooks.pub/rhetoricineverydaylife/chapter/logic-is-it-logical-by-mica-giberti/.

Chapter 3

Present and captivate your global audience

When you are presenting to a culturally diverse group of people, you will face multiple challenges – language barriers, values differences, verbal and nonverbal messages with different meanings, etc. In a cross-cultural situation, your common sense may not be so common.

How do you most effectively Adapt so that your message is crystal clear, unique, and memorable – and yet universally resonates with audience across cultures?

I'll show you the step-by-step strategy to develop a persuasive presentation, so that your message will be not only clearly heard but also acted upon despite the cultural diversity in the audience.

When You Say Everything, You Say Nothing

When I competed in Toastmasters international speech contest for the first time, I met Janice – an athletic-looking Caribbean lady in her mid-50s with bright eyes and an assertive demeanor. At the semifinal round of the New York district, Janice was sitting all the way at the back.

As soon as my name was announced as the winner, she came over to me and said,

"You have potential. Let me coach you."

I thought, *How generous of her to offer me free coaching! OK, it'll be good practice.*

Little did I know that her coaching would completely change the way I think about public speaking.

I thought my speech was pretty good.

So all I had to do was to rehearse!

In my seven-minute speech, I included *everything* I wanted to say.

If you imagine a grand buffet, they have everything from appetizers to steaks, fish, pasta, veggies, desserts, and fruits. You may not be able to eat everything, but everyone will definitely have something to pick!

DOI: 10.4324/9781003455615-4

The Toastmasters' audience is quite diverse. I don't know what each of them is interested in. Just like a grand buffet, I should offer everything I got. Something's gotta stick. This way, everyone in the audience can pick and choose from a large array of messages and learnings they want to take away. Everyone will be happy. Right?

Wrong!

I prided myself as a content-rich speaker.

In my first session with Janice, however, my grand buffet was completely torn apart, to a one-dish à la carte.

Janice said,

"If your audience takes away different messages, your speech is a failure. What is ONE thing you really want them to remember, and remember well?"

This was eye-opening for me.

I always thought a great speaker is a content-rich speaker.

But if you put yourself in the audience's shoes, too much content will only confuse them.

Imagine, as soon as you as an audience member begin to start writing something down, the speaker would say something else worth noting and you can't catch it. Because the speaker shares so many points, you can't recall any of them.

Especially in a cross-cultural situation, the audience's interpretation of your messages may be different. The more content you offer, the higher chance that your diverse audience will receive varied messages, only to make your presentation confusing – and less memorable.

In the previous chapter, we learned One BIG Message®.

No matter what kind of presentation or speech or other form of communication, there is always one important point that you want the audience to take away.

That's your One BIG Message.

And you need to convey this One BIG Message throughout your communication consistently.

Just one. Because not all information is made equal.

Let me explain.

There is some information that's more focused on your big idea and other bits that contain more details, like supporting evidence or examples. Your big idea is One BIG Message, and details that support your One BIG Message are Main Points.

One BIG Message example

Let's consider an example:

Meet one of my coaching clients, Mayuna, who entered the Mrs. International Beauty Pageant.

You might think that a beauty pageant is all about swimsuits and glamour. Confession: I thought that, too! However, each contestant is responsible for delivering a 30-second speech. The goal of this speech is basically a self-introduction. The contestant talks about their life achievements, values, charity involvements, etc., with the hope of convincing judges that they deserve to be crowned. And in fact, the speech accounts for 50% of the judging criteria. Who knew?

I worked with Mayuna to find her One BIG Message to convey an easy-to-understand – yet punchy, memorable – message that would engage her global audience in 30 seconds.

Mayuna is a life coach, and she already had a huge accumulation of achievements with so much life experience. The process was like trying to find the golden nugget.

Most of my clients struggle with this initial process. They have so much to offer, they don't know where to start. That's why, in the first session of my global presentation training, I spend a lot of time listening to the client's story, ask strategic questions, and dig deeper into their past experiences, values, and feelings until we find that "golden nugget." It could be a little moment you didn't realize was important.

The key to successful communication is to find a point of contact between "your own perspective" and the "their perspective."

When that point of contact is found, we can Adapt our message by narrowing down on the key information, scraping off what doesn't resonate with them, then zero in on the message concisely to ten words or fewer.

Again, less is more.

That's One BIG Message.

Searching for the right One BIG Message is like panning for gold.

Looking back on the past 30 or even 40 years of life and crafting a speech to make the judges, whom you're meeting for the first time, understand you best and stand out from other contestants. And all of this in just 30 seconds.

As you might imagine, it's not a task that can be completed overnight. You might feel lost, unsure of what to convey or where to even begin. Particularly in pageants like Mrs. International, Mayuna needed to stand out among 50 other contestants all representing their own countries.

When searching for the One BIG Message, the most crucial process is "introspection."

Mayuna has supported over 1,000 clients as a life coach, so she is not only skilled in guiding clients through introspection but is also accustomed to reflecting on herself regularly. That was very helpful in our search for her one and only One BIG Message.

During the initial personal session, she had already shared around ten pages of content, roughly 4,000 characters, all typed up in a very organized fashion in Microsoft Word. Using this as a foundation, by delving deeper into our conversations and questions, she would unearth or expand upon moments that hadn't occurred to her before.

Have you ever gone gold panning? You might have seen it or even tried it.

When gold panning, you first aim for a spot where gold might be, scoop up the sand, and carefully sift through it. Then, you might exclaim, "Ah! Something shiny appeared!"

Searching for the One BIG Message is akin to gold panning.

Amidst the wealth of information you want to convey and the numerous events in your life, you search for that shining gem that encapsulates it all. To do this, you start by brainstorming all your thoughts and capturing the big picture.

This isn't something easily done alone. Engaging in dialogues with a coach or a trusted individual deepens and broadens the big picture, increasing the likelihood of discovering those shining golden nuggets.

Of course, not everyone is as adept at introspection as Mayuna. Most of my clients struggle with this initial process. That's why, during the first coaching session, I focus on listening, empathizing, and facilitating the client's thoughts, helping to deepen and expand them.

Narrowing down the message

Once the broad and deep image comes into view, you start searching for the "gold" while sifting through the whole.

The point where many falter is the "listener's perspective."

While uncovering a message only you can convey, it's crucial not to focus solely on that but to find the common ground between your perspective and the listener's perspective – in this case, the judges and organizers of Mrs. International. It's key to consider if choosing you would be beneficial for Mrs. International.

Once you find that connection, you preserve the essential information and eliminate the rest, then proceed to articulate the message – your One BIG Message.

If your One BIG Message is too long, it won't be memorable. Aim for simple, concise, and clear expression – around ten words in English. If it's in Japanese, I recommend 20 characters or fewer. It could be different in your language. Think of the most memorable catchphrase in advertisements in your language. I bet they are "short" in your language.

After our deep conversation, Mayuna and I came up with her One BIG Message as follows:

"Follow your heart" (three words).

with a variation of:

"Following your heart is the best way to find your own way" (12 words).

When you have a one-of-a-kind One BIG Message, it also creates a ripple effect.

Mayuna started to use her One BIG Message with her clients to help them follow their hearts. Her friends started to use her One BIG Message, too, and said, "Hey Mayuna, don't be nervous at the beauty pageant! Just follow your heart!"

Your One BIG Message is not just for one-time use. When it's powerful enough, it becomes your brand. It leaves a lasting legacy.

Because your One BIG Message is *adapted* to their perspectives, your message will be consistently heard and acted upon.

Build on the One BIG Message

Every piece of information you include in your speech should be selected carefully with the goal of conveying this One BIG Message.

The next step is to build depth to this One BIG Message – an emotionally resonating story with a persuasive and logical structure that can vividly convey the One BIG Message, with a captivating opening and a long-lasting closing.

Let's start with a structure.

Generally, the structure of a speech is often based on the opening, body, and closing.

However, to truly engage your audience's hearts and minds, this traditional structure is often insufficient. Notably successful speakers like Steve Jobs and former U.S. President Obama don't just limit themselves to these three stages; they intricately refine their structure even further.

To captivate your audience's hearts and minds, it's essential to strategically embed information in a detailed manner, but all this information must be interconnected, flowing not just as individual "points" but as a continuous "line."

Enabling this is what I call the "9-Step Structure" in the Breakthrough Method®.

The 9-Step Structure

Breakthrough Method uses this principle to structure the entire speech or presentation. I call it the "9-Step Structure."

1. Opening: preview One BIG Message
2. Transition into the first Main Point
3. First Main Point

4. Tie into One BIG Message, and transition into the second Main Point
5. Second Main Point
6. Tie into One BIG Message, and Transition into the third Main Point
7. Third Main Point
8. Tie into One BIG Message, and transition into closing
9. Closing

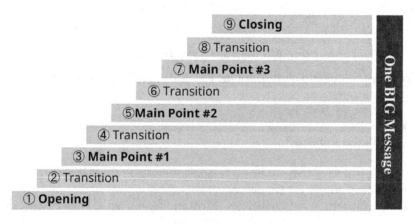

Illustration of a presentation structure

Now that you are equipped with the foundational logical thinking technique in the previous chapter, it's time to lay out your messages in a presentation format.

The 9-Step Structure helps you make your speech persuasive and memorable, every time.

Let me break it down.

This 9-Step Structure has three important points.

First, *One BIG Message.*

Second, there are *three Main Points* to support One BIG Message.

Third, in between each point, there is always a *transition.*

Let me start with the first point.

One BIG Message

We already learned what One BIG Message is. But I can't emphasize the importance of One BIG Message enough.

Every single element in your speech is strategically placed to convey this One BIG Message. Just *one.*

One BIG Message becomes the through line that you keep returning to when you craft your presentation.

Here is a pitfall.

One BIG Message is *not* just the message *you* as a speaker want to convey.

It has to be something your *audience* resonates with.

I call it the "You-Focused" message.

It may be easy to say, "Think about your audience when developing your message."

But in reality, it's even easier to think from your point of view, or "I-Focused" message.

Always make your One BIG Message "You-Focused"

So before coming up with your One BIG Message, it is critical that you ask these four questions.

The first question is:

1. Who's the audience?

> Don't just say, "My audience is single women in their 30s who live in New York City." Go deeper.
> Ask yourself: What challenges, frustrations, interests, voids, flaws, do they have? What are their pain points?

The second question is:

2. What's in it for them?

> Why should they listen to you? If they didn't receive your message, what might happen to them? Put yourself in their shoes.

The third question is:

3. Why you?

> This is the question most speakers don't ask. But this question is very important.
> Are you replaceable? Hopefully not. You want your audience to see you as the only speaker who can deliver your message. What's your knowledge, experience, values, vision, or resources that qualify you to speak on this topic?
> Clarify that.

The fourth question is:

4. How do you want them to think, feel, and act differently as a result?

What is the exact next step you want your audience to take after your speech?

Think about a micro goal for each and every time you give a presentation.

Throughout your speech crafting process, always come back to these questions.

Now, you are ready to develop your one and only One BIG Message.

Develop your unique One BIG Message

Many of my clients ask me, "Does my One BIG Message have to be a new idea that my audience has never heard of?"

My answer is: *no.*

Your message itself may be similar to others.

But what makes you, and your One BIG Message unique, is your own perspectives, your own personal stories, and your own unique way of delivering it.

How can you say it in your own unique words? How can you add "you-ism"?

Develop supporting Main Points

To support your One BIG Message, you will also need some details, reasons, background, or stories to support your One BIG Message. These are called Main Points. This is my second point about the 9-Step Structure.

In the 9-Step Structure, you see three Main Points.

Why three?

Well, let's watch the first minute of this video. You may have seen this famous speech before. It's Steve Jobs' 2005 Stanford commencement address. Just watch the first minute.

https://youtu.be/UF8uR6Z6KLc

Welcome back.

"Today, I'm gonna tell you three stories of my life. That's it."

Not only Steve Jobs, but many experienced speakers use the "Power of 3."

Three is the magic number.

If you provide only one or two Main Points, or stories, that's not enough content. The audience won't be fully convinced. But if you provide four, five, or even more, that's too much content. They will recall nothing.

Remember, If you say everything, you say nothing.

So you need three Main Points to support your One BIG Message.

These Main Points are details, reasons, backgrounds, examples, facts, or stories to support your One BIG Message.

What Main Points do you want your audience to have, so they can "get" your main message?

A frequently overlooked element in presentations

Now, you've probably watched many speakers go from one Main Point to another by stating something like, "OK, now, point number 1 is . . ." or "Now, my next point is . . . ."

Right?

This leads to my third point about the 9-Step Structure.

In between each Main Point, you always need a *transition*.

This is by far one of the most neglected parts of a presentation.

Those speakers take for granted that the audience is still with them and the audience wants to move on to this next point at your timing.

You might know it's a valuable point – but how will they know?

If you are only giving them bullet points in your talk, just write them down in an e-mail and send it to them.

As a speaker, you need to elicit their emotion.

Transitions can completely breathe new life into a speech and get your audience leaning forward waiting to hear what comes next.

Transitions can do these two things:

1. Remind the audience where they were with the point you just made.
2. Notice the audience to join you on the journey to the next point.

In another words, it's a tease, so your audience will think, "I can't wait to hear what's coming up!"

Let's watch this segment of my TEDx Talk to show you what I mean. Just watch this segment: 8:10 ~ 9:10.

https://www.youtube.com/watch?v=pzYrw7apHGc&t=51s

Welcome back.

Did you hear how I went back to my incident with Freshman Nate, and summarized learnings before moving on to the next story?

Did you also notice how I enticed them to come along and teased them with what's coming next?

Here's a suggestion for you.

If you're going to memorize your opening line of your speech and your closing statements, remember to memorize and internalize your transitions as well.

Do not wing them. They're way too important!

To keep the audience engaged and wanting more, you need to connect all the dots to One BIG Message.

Think about what you can say to transition to the next point, so you can keep them engaged.

Pyramid structure between One BIG Message and Main Points

In reality, when you are developing your business presentation, you will most likely have multiple Main Points, or research findings first. Then you will draw your One BIG Message. Before you can present your idea to your team, top management or client, you still need to first check "So What?" and "Why So?" between your One BIG Message and each Main Point.

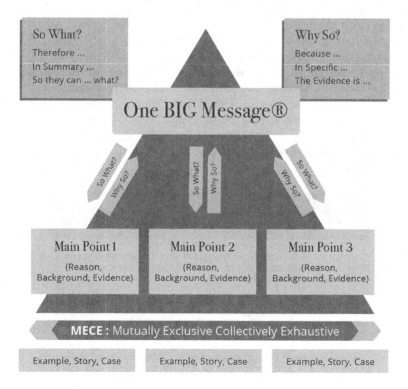

Pyramid structure, the foundation of logical thinking

As we learned in Chapter 2, "So What?" and "Why So?" are two critical questions to craft your message strategically.

The first question – "So What?" – clarifies the logical connection between each of your Main Points and your One BIG Message. Your Main Points are the facts, data, research findings, and statements that you use to back up your One BIG Message. These Main Points are the middle level of information in the pyramid structure, and all Main Points should be Mutually Exclusive Collectively Exhaustive (MECE).

What is this Main Point actually telling us? Why should your audience care? Here are the Main Points. Therefore . . . What?

Look at the arrow pointing from Main Points to One BIG Message. Bottom up. By asking "So What?", they can . . . what, you can check whether your Main Point logically explains your One BIG Message.

The second question, "Why So?", goes the other direction – from One BIG Message to Main Points. Your overall message is your One BIG Message.

Why did you come to such a conclusion? In other words, "Why So?"

Check the logical connection again between One BIG Message and each Main Point, but this time, top-down.

Let's put it in practice.

Take a look at this case.

Pretend that you are working for a pasta sauce company.

In your research, you found these trends among competitors A, B, and C. What One BIG Message can you draw from these findings?

Make sure that you ask "So What?" and "Why So?" between your One BIG Message, and each finding about competitors A, B, and C.

Pasta sauce competitive analysis case

You researched competitive landscape of the pasta sauce market. You found out the followings about market's top three competitors A, B, and C. What One Big Message can you draw from these findings?

Competitor A: Sales have been growing at a rate of 17% annually since 2017. Especially Asian-flavored pasta sauces have been doing well among millennials through online shops.

Competitor B: In the past few years, Italian grandma's heirloom tomato sauces have grown rapidly to make up more than half of this company's overall sales, contributing to the total revenue growth of this company. Their core target is Gen X with families, who buy these products in a large supermarket chains.

Competitor C: About 40% of their sales are derived from the various mushroom sauces with a Michelin star chef's recipe, compared to 25% two years ago. Sales channel is also limited to high end gourmet stores, and they are doing extremely well among busy working moms in metropolitan cities.

Description of the pasta sauce case

Take a pause, and think about the One BIG Message you can draw from these research findings.

What One BIG Message did you come up with?

Does your One BIG Message cover all facts found in the research, with no leaping, overlooking, or going off the point in the logic?

Let's take a look.

If you look at A, B, and C, you should be able to find something in common.

First, all three companies have increased their sales of the pasta sauces in question.

Second, all the findings include information about products, target consumers, and channels.

Company A's core products are Asian-flavored pasta sauces.

Company B's core products are Italian grandma's heirloom tomato sauces.

Company C's core products are various mushroom sauces with a Michelin star chef's recipe.

All of these products have unique product positioning.

How about their target consumers?

Company A's target is millennials.

Company B's target is Gen X families.

Company C's target is working moms.

Clear targeting.

Channels.

Company A sells their core products through online shops.

Company B sells their core products in large supermarket chains.

Company C sells their core products in high-end gourmet stores in metropolitan cities.

They all have strong focus on clearly differentiated channels.

Let's look at the One BIG Message you came up with.

If your One BIG Message looks something like,

"Competitors are growing their sales with clear targeting."

You are close, but you are only looking at "target consumers."

Let's use "So What?" and "Why So?".

"Competitors are growing their sales with clear targeting."

→ Why So? Because of clear product positioning, targeting, and channels.

→ Companies have clear product positioning, targeting, and channels.

→ So What? Competitors are growing their sales with clear targeting . . . .

You can see that you are overlooking product positioning and channels, right?

So your One BIG Message doesn't sound quite as persuasive.

If your One BIG Message is something like

"Pasta sauces are becoming more popular."

You have a leap in your logic – probably off-track, too – because research findings only talk about companies A, B, and C, and you don't know how other company's pasta sauces are doing.

They may not necessarily be "popular," *and* your core research finding is about sales growth and what contributed to the growth.

So focusing on popularity is off-track.

You will see that clearly when you ask "So What?" and "Why So?".

"Pasta sauces are becoming more popular."

→ Why So? Because of clear product positioning, targeting, and channels.
→ Companies have clear product positioning, targeting, and channels.
→ So What? So "Pasta sauces are becoming more popular."

Now you see the leap, and off-track, right?

So what does a logically sound One BIG Message sound like?

How about this?

"The Sales growth of top three competitors is largely attributed to unique differentiation in product positioning, targeting, and sales channels."

Check using "So What?" and "Why So?" with this One BIG Message, and each of the findings about companies A, B, and C.

No leap, no overlook, and no veering off-track. Right?

Only by asking "So What?" and "Why So?" can you can come up with a clear, logically sound message.

This process may be tedious to you at first, but going through this process – or not – determines whether your audience will buy into your message – or not. As you make it your habit to always ask "So What?" and "Why So?", it gets faster, easier, and more efficient.

So make sure that you ask "So What?" and "Why So?" every time you think you have your sound One BIG Message and the Main Points to support it.

Now, think about your own speech or presentation that you are planning to give, or you've given in the past.

What is your One BIG Message?

Is your One BIG Message high level enough, but not too high to be vague?

Is your One BIG Message simple enough? Crystal clear?

Are there any other messages that you thought would be helpful but only making them indigestible for your audience?

And what are the Main Points that you'll use to support your One BIG Message?

Right them down on a piece of paper, and do the "So What?" "Why So?" check.

If you find any leap, overlook, or if you start to go off-track, go back to your messages. You may need to tweak them. Keep adjusting your One BIG Message and Main Points, so that they are all logically sound in all directions.

When you think you have decided on your One BIG Message, always ask yourself, "So What?" "Why So?" or "So they can . . . What?" "Why can you say so?" Not once, not twice – as many times as you need to in order to gain the true value for your audience.

By now, you have created your One BIG Message and Main Points, the logical backbone of your global presentation.

In order to influence people and move them to action, you have to be able to trigger their emotions – Pathos – and there is no better way to do that than to tell a compelling story. Stories are the universal language. Especially in a cross-cultural situation, stories unite people's hearts.

Before you sell anything, you need your audience to connect with you. They need to understand your Why and identify with you on a more personal level.

The Why is your story.

But here is the thing. Very few leaders know how to articulate their Why, their reason for being and why anyone should even care. They don't have a formula to develop a story in a systematic way.

But you do.

Let me introduce you to the storytelling formula, that works every time even before a culturally diverse audience – The 6Cs of Strategic Storytelling.

Convey your One BIG message in a story to connect with your audience

Connections and meaningful relationships are crucial in life. It's true in business, too. They're the foundation for sustained partnerships and successful collaborations, whether it be with your team, your leaders, your clients, or other stakeholders.

Whether or not we're able to acknowledge it, each of us carries an innate need to connect with other people. We all desire to be liked, heard, and understood. That's human nature. But why is it that some people seem to build instant rapport with almost anyone they come across?

If you want to really improve your power of persuasion and get any audience to connect with you, take a look at some of the following ways you can bond with your audience.

Listen

It's impossible to establish connection if you don't listen. This means finding out what your audience is interested in, not interested in, struggling with, happy with, frustrated with, etc.

Contact some of the people in the audience beforehand and ask them what they're struggling with right now, what they want to learn more about, and how you can add value. It's much better to find out these things in advance rather than afterwards. If it's not possible to connect with your audience directly one-on-one beforehand, there are other ways to gain insights to inform your talk. You can research online about the specific event, the particular industry, or the participants' companies. The event organizer can also be a great resource for information, as they're likely tuned into their attendees on a deeper level.

Get personal

If you really want to create a deep and meaningful connection with your audience, you must make it personal. People will respect your honesty if they can see your vulnerability and not just a polished performance.

Deliver your One BIG Message in a story

When you wrap up your One BIG Message in a story, you are making it much easier for your audience to relate to and recall afterwards. Introduce characters that your audience are most likely to relate to. Use dialogue that's familiar to them – and if possible, make your audience a character in your story.

The 6Cs of Strategic Storytelling

Now, how can we wrap your One BIG Message up in a story effectively?

I have developed the effective storytelling framework called "The 6Cs of Strategic Storytelling" so you can develop a compelling story every single time – not matter what topic, no matter who your audience is.

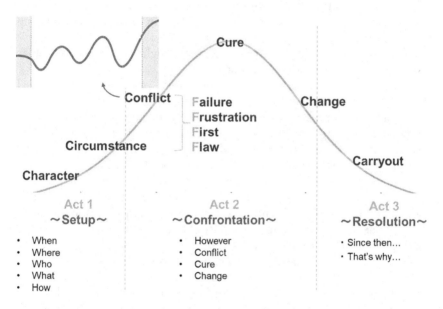

The 6Cs of Strategic Storytelling

The 6Cs of Strategic Storytelling are based on the three-act structure, often used in screenplay writing.[1]

Act 1 is setup. It's used for exposition – to establish the main characters, their relationships, and the world they live in.

Act 2 is confrontation. Some tough incident occurs, and confronts the main character. The main character attempts to resolve the conflict, only to find themselves in ever worsening situations. They must learn new skills or come to some revelation about themselves and their lives.

Act 3 is resolution. It features the resolution of the story, leaving the characters with a new sense of who they really are.

Think of the plot of your favorite movie. I'm sure it follows this three-act structure.

Corporate storytelling goes the same way; however, there is one big difference.

It's the next step.

In films and other forms of entertainment, the main goal is to leave the audience with some feelings, but afterwards the audience will go back to their own lives and do their own things in their own ways.

In business, our main goal is to leave the audience with a motivation to take specific action that's expected of them. The specific action may be "buy this product" or "register online" or simply "make a next meeting appointment."

Whatever your expected "specific action" might be, corporate stories must lead the audience to the next step.

So before you choose a topic for your story, make sure you clarified the specific next step you want your audience to take. With that in mind, choose an appropriate episode. Just because you thought about a certain episode off the top of your head or experienced something interesting recently doesn't mean that is the right episode to convey your One BIG Message and lead your audience to take the "specific action."

You need to go back in time, dig out your past – sometimes the past you may not want to tap into – and explore your experience to find the right episode to build story from. Sounds challenging? Here is a suggestion for you.

Create a "story bank" and start collecting stories.

You could use an Excel sheet, like I do, or use a notebook.

When interesting situations happen, make a note of them.

When you come across interesting people, take a visual picture in your head. These people will eventually become your characters, and the daily situations you find yourself in will form a narrative that will help you tell your story.

Some of the situations you find yourself in may not seem interesting at first, but when you need to make a point to your audience, you can draw on them.

The 6Cs of Strategic Storytelling will help you turn these situations into great stories and leave a lasting legacy.

So let's dive in.

Character

What do you remember most about a story? It's usually the people in it.

Circumstances or situations become interesting because there is a relatable character within them.

Every story has a main character, called the hero or protagonist.

Many stories have a bad guy: the villain or antagonist.

You might play the hero or the protagonist, but make your story real, not fictional – otherwise, it won't be relatable. Clearly crafted characters make your story believable and help to build an emotional connection with your audience. Bring your characters to life so your audience can "see," "hear," and "feel" them.

For example, they may have distinctive appearances (including body language, tone of voice, or mannerisms) that you can draw out in your speech (and you can even become that character).

Reveal just two or three carefully chosen details when introducing a character. You are not an actor, after all. You are a speaker.

Also highlight your characters' inner motivation. What do they want? What do they *not* want?

What are their goals, and what's standing in the way of those goals? That character will then come alive for your audience, and they'll be emotionally hooked into your story.

Circumstance

When crafting a good story, there needs to be a narrative – a circumstance that gives the story some context. It needs to take your listeners on a journey that will lead them to an insight or realization.

Circumstance is the "before" picture. What were things like before the protagonist takes a journey in the story? Paint that picture clearly here, so that later in the story, it is clear for the audience to see the "before" and "after."

Something then happens in your story which starts a series of events that draw out the scenario you want your audience to buy into, leading to the *after*math. The best stories draw on a personal experience, rather than a fictional story. This helps to build credibility and authority.

Think of a moment in your life that led to your success as a leader. Even more interesting is what failures you've experienced along the way. They show vulnerability and make an audience buy into you. Your audience need to understand Why your story is being told. Why is it important *now*? Make it relevant and timely to them in the *here* and *now*.

Conflict

Conflict is perhaps the most important part of story because it creates tension, and gives your audience a reason to care and "stay in the room." Look into what I call "4Fs" to create conflict:

Failure, Flaw, Frustration, and First.

Did the main character attempt to do something but fail? What flaw did he/she have to overcome? What was he/she frustrated with? What happened when he/she tried something for the first time? These are the conflicts you want to highlight in your story, because this is where your audience feel: "I've been there. This person gets me."

Here is a tip when introducing a conflict. Don't show a conflict in one shot. Elevate the conflict little by little. I call it, the "Mall Escalator" method.

With mall escalators, you go up one flight, walk around the floor, then go up another flight, right? Just like that, you want to create emotional escalation – plateau – escalation – plateau . . . .

This way, you can shake up audience's emotion, and create suspense.

If you take the movie *Titanic* as an example, after the ship hits the iceberg, the conflict rises little by little, like the "Mall Escalator" way.

If the ship sinks as soon as she hits the iceberg, the story ends right there.

I call it the "Elevator Method." Taking you from the ground floor directly to your destination floor. Done.

On the other hand, if the water only penetrates the lower deck and the ship doesn't sink at all, the story never ends.

I call it the "Moving Walkway Method." You know one of those flat escalator things you see at airports? It's flat all the way. No excitement at all. This is a recipe for boredom.

Remember that your audience is hardwired to pay attention to the problems in a story.

The moment you mention a trap, a failure, a mistake – *boom!* You're in, and you've got your audience hooked.

Do this well, and you'll create an experience they'll remember long after they hear you speak.

Consider the problems, challenges, or fears members of your audience face and weave those into the story to make it as relevant and personal as possible.

Cure

The cure is the climatic part of your story, that causes a positive shift in the main character's life, situation, or values. The cure is the solution or revelation. Cure could be a person, a thing, or an incident.

But . . . you, the speaker, cannot be the cure. Never make yourself a guru. Why? Because the audience wants to see that you're the one who learned a lesson so that they can take your advice to experience an improved situation themselves like you. What was the cure that caused you to overcome the conflict you were facing?

Share that with your audience, and perhaps it might just be what they need to help them overcome their own challenges.

Change

In great stories, the protagonist is never the same at the end as they were at the beginning.

They must change as a result of the conflict. At the end, they might be kind, more resilient, wiser, and stronger. Your presentation must take a similar journey so your audience understands the key piece of wisdom or advice that allowed them to overcome their obstacles and change for the better. This key takeaway message could then be packaged into a short, memorable phrase or sound bite that could easily become viral on social media platforms following the event.

Carryout

Last, but not least.

What is the single most important piece of information or concept that you want your audience to leave with? What action do you want them to take as a result of your story? What lessons can be learned? Your lasting key takeaway should be simple enough to be remembered and easy enough for them to go away and implement. And this is where you would lead your audience toward the next step they should be taking.

Now that you learned all of the 6Cs as a framework, let's look at some examples.

Stacey Abrams' speech at the 2019 State of the Union address

When former Georgia Democratic gubernatorial candidate Stacey Abrams delivered the Democratic response to then-U.S. President Donald Trump's 2019 State of the Union address (https://youtu.be/5aFT0OHmiqc), she used one powerful tool throughout her speech – storytelling.

In case you are not too familiar with Stacey Abrams, she was the 2018 Democratic gubernatorial candidate, and after losing the Georgia governor's race and allegations of voter suppression, she devoted her efforts to improving this situation. Abrams formed an organization to register and empower voters, wrote a book about voter suppression, and co-produced a documentary, *All In: The Fight for Democracy*. In the 2020 election, her relentless efforts paid off.

Throughout her book and documentary, she uses the power of story, but her speech at the 2019 State of the Union address sums it all up.

First, Abrams' One BIG Message was clear throughout this speech:

"Together, we are coming for America, for a better America."

She brings her personal story about her family; in particular her father's story as a through line in her speech to strengthen her One BIG Message.

Let me explain how strategically she did it based on "The 6Cs of Strategic Storytelling."

Character

In her opening, she introduces her parents:
Her librarian mother, who taught her to love learning.
Her shipyard worker father, who put in overtime and extra shifts.
And that they made sure they volunteered to help others.
Both parents emphasized family values, which were faith, service, education, and responsibility. These values led Stacey Abrams to serve the country she loves, with a strong belief that coming together beyond differences is crucial for the greater good of this country.

Circumstance

Her family went back and forth between lower middle class and working poor.
Since her family was poor, they only had one car, so sometimes her dad had to hitchhike and walk 30 miles home from the shipyards.
One rainy night, when her father didn't come home, everyone in her family gets in the car and goes out looking for him – and eventually finds him making his way along the road, soaked and shivering in his shirtsleeves.
Mother asks if he'd left his coat at work. He explains he'd given it to a homeless man he'd met on the highway. That was his only jacket. Father turns to his family and says, "I knew when I left that man, he'd still be alone. But I could give him my coat, because I knew you were coming for me."
This beautiful story is short, yet extremely impactful.
First, "Rainy night," "soaking wet," "shivering in shirtsleeves" give us vivid visual image and we can even feel and smell the cold rain. When telling a story, you want to touch your audience's visual, auditorial, and kinetic senses to bring the story to life vividly.
Second, she uses a dialogue ("father says to me, "[father's line]," instead of "father told me that I should . . . ."). This makes her father come alive in the story, and these lines are enough to spotlight his personalities and values. You can even act out the character by highlighting interesting features that character has.
Third, this short story she tells in her opening introduces her family values that were handed down to her, and she strategically sets up a foundation for her One BIG Message: "Together, we are coming for America, for a better America," and contrasts with upcoming conflict. Remember, the reason why you are telling a story is to make your One BIG Message memorable.

Conflict

Then, Stacey Abrams describes not one, not two, but countless conflicts America is facing, including challenges with educational cost, gun safety measures, immigration plan, climate change, the Affordable Care Act, looming layoffs, closing plants, wages struggling to keep pace with the cost of living, and many hard-working Americans falling behind, living paycheck to paycheck.

Most importantly, voter suppression. From making it harder to register and stay on the rolls to moving and closing polling places to rejecting lawful ballots, Abrams stresses that we can no longer ignore these threats to democracy.

Abrams is extremely skilled in showing conflicts. In order to emotionally connect with listeners, conflicts shouldn't be shown in one shot. Stack up the conflict one after another and create the emotional escalation. Remember the "Mall Escalator" method?

Abrams is using the "Mall Escalator" method to effectively shake up the listener's emotions.

Don't use the "Elevator Method" or "Moving Walkway Method."

Cure

Cure is the changemaker. It's the climatic finish of the story. Cure could be a person, a thing, or an incident that becomes the catalyst for positive change.

In Abrams' case, she uses her father's credo as Cure – together, we are coming for America, for a better America. And Abrams stress her point that when America shares this belief, "Change" will happen.

Change

In many stories, the main character and their situation change for the better as a result of overcoming their conflicts.

In Abrams' case, she describes the foreseeable "Change" – a "better America" if "America comes together."

> Our power and strength as Americans live in our hard work and our belief in more. My family understood firsthand that while success is not guaranteed, we live in a nation where opportunity is possible. But we do not succeed alone – in these United States, when times are tough, we can persevere because our friends and neighbors will come for us. Our first responders will come for us.

Carryout

In closing, Abrams calls for action – exercise your voting rights. Stand for, and with one another, for stronger America together.

"Carryout," or the takeaway message is this: "we will create a stronger America, *together*."

She brings back her family values and emphasizes that America wins by fighting for our shared values against all enemies, foreign and domestic. That is who we are – and when we do so, never wavering, the state of our union will always be strong.

How Mayuna turned her One BIG Message into a story with her authentic voice

Remember Mayuna, the beauty pageant contestant and my coaching client?

After we developed her One BIG Message, "Follow Your Heart," it was time to start fleshing it out using The 6Cs of Strategic Storytelling so that she could really engage with the global audience and keep them hooked.

I helped her create characters so that they can be seen, felt, and heard, and a narrative that got the audience always wanting more.

It was really important that the narrative sounded like it was coming from her voice and didn't sound "borrowed" from someone else. I helped her find different expressions to make sure they sounded authentic to her, as though she has really lived the experience.

We did this work carefully to every corner of her speech. This process is like picking up and polishing each golden nugget.

For the pageant, we prepared a 60-second version and a 30-second version. The 60-second version has 112 words in 55 seconds, and the 30-second version has 73 words in 27 seconds, refined down from her original 4,000 words' worth of material. This shows how concise you have to be to communicate your One BIG Message firmly.

It doesn't matter whether your speech is for a beauty pageant, a board presentation, or a room full of international leaders, the process is the same.

Four Secrets that will help you tell captivating stories

As human beings, we are hardwired to be storytellers. We also love hearing stories. It gives us an emotional connection between the characters in the story and the audience.

Studies have shown that when people are shown statistics and then a story, only 5% remembered the stats, but 63% remembered the story.

Sometimes, however, we forget to bring the use of storytelling into the business arena. Maybe we feel that they can't be factual enough. Yet the truth is, your audience aren't looking for another sales pitch, they want to be captivated by a story that changes their thinking and causes them to take action.

Here are my four secrets that will help you tell captivating stories that persuade your audience.

1. Focus on the struggle more than the success

Have you noticed that whenever you hear a great business leader speak, they rarely talk about their success? That would be too immodest. They focus their story on the effort, or struggle, more than the success itself.

The reason is because effort is more relatable than success. We all go through some sort of struggle to achieve what we want, to varying degrees, and this is what makes the characters and storyline far more interesting.

You can use your story's hero to communicate the struggle, and introduce a mentor character to help them overcome it.

2. Know who you are talking to

You need to know your audience if you want your message to resonate with them. It's no good talking about something that's not going or be relevant to the challenges your audience are currently facing.

Too many speakers prepare material with their own perspective in mind, without walking in their audience's shoes and understanding their needs. When you create a story that resonates with the audience, you're creating a subtext which is: "I get you. I understand your world."

This instantly gets your audience on side and encourages them to listen and stay engaged in what you have to say.

3. Create an obstacle

In The 6Cs of Strategic Storytelling, I call this the "conflict." It's part of the hero's journey and is the cause of what's stopping them from achieving his or her goal. It has to be something your audience can deeply connect to, and that has relevance and value to them.

The conflict or obstacle should be resolved in the story by what you have to offer, whether it be a physical product or service.

4. Add a twist

The best stories always have an element of surprise. It could be a good surprise or a bad one. Whatever you choose, make it unexpected.

Your story could be about a famous person, but only revealing their identity at the end.

Tell a story when things were going so well (after a struggle) but then take a turn for the worse.

Give an unlikely connection between two people or two events that the audience don't expect.

You can incorporate humor and dialogue to help you deliver the element of surprise, as this helps to keep your audience's interest – which can make your story unforgettable!

Three steps before you start telling your stories

Storytelling has become a must-have leadership skill. It gives you the power to change opinion and behavior, to persuade and motivate and connect your people with your vision.

Leaders who have sharpened their storytelling skills are able to better engage employees, recruit better, create distinct competitive positioning, have a stronger corporate culture, and deliver a positive investment return.

But you don't have to be a superhero to deliver powerful stories, but you do need the right tools and processes.

The 6Cs of Strategic Storytelling you just learned in this chapter will help you become more authentic, meaningful, and powerful by communicating your messages using storytelling. Whether you are delivering a speech, presentation, sales pitch, or just speaking up in meetings, The 6Cs of Strategic Storytelling framework is ideal if you want to become more influential and powerfully persuasive in global business.

But I need to be honest with you.

Persuading with a story is hard. But following are three steps to take, so you can make a good start.

Step 1: start collecting stories

To be a good storyteller, you need to start collecting stories. When interesting situations happen, make a note of them. When you come across interesting people, take a visual picture in your head. These people will eventually become your characters and the daily situations you find yourself in will form a narrative that will help you communicate your messages.

Some of the situations you find yourself in may not seem interesting at first, but then when you need to make a point to your audience, you can draw on them. It's like having your own playbook of stories.

The 6Cs of Strategic Storytelling will help you turn these situations into great stories and leave a lasting legacy.

Step 2: analyze stories

Now that you've started collecting interesting stories, start analyzing them. Do any of the characters resonate with you? Do you empathize with them? What made the characters take specific actions? The more analytical you can be with situations and people around you, the more you'll start to become a better storyteller.

Step 3: Test your stories

Tell your story to a test audience. Ask them how the story makes them feel, and what they remember. What do they take away when they hear your story? This will help to see whether you're making your points effectively.

Having a great story in your head is one thing, but telling it in an engaging and persuasive way is quite another! So make sure you test your stories before taking a big stage.

Your turn

Now that you learned all 6Cs, saw specific examples, and learned some secrets to help you become a powerful storyteller in business, it's your turn to map out your story.

First, what is the point you are trying to make, and what episode/topic/story would best describe it?

Second, what's the exact next step you want them to take, and how would you end your story so you can lead into the next step?

Third and finally, write down each element of the 6Cs.

When crafting a story, you'll need to describe the characters' appearance, emotions, and auditory sensations – but be cautious not to get too detailed, as an overly detailed description can make the story drag. Make sure that your conflict comes in stages – the Mall Escalator method. Think about the 4Fs to source your conflict – Failure, Frustration, Flaw, First. Even if you have one big conflict, you can still divide it up into a few segments so that you can create the wave of emotional escalation and plateau.

The 7–30 rule and six ways to open your global presentation with a bang!

First impressions matter.

This is true not only in a dating situation, but also when you are speaking.

Did you know that within the first seven seconds of your speech, your audience will have formed an impression of you? And within 30 seconds, they will have decided whether or not they want to hear more from you?

I call it the 7–30 rule.

Yet, most speakers open with something like,

"Thank you so much for having me here."

"I'm truly honored to be speaking to you today."

"First, let me acknowledge our sponsors."

If you were in the audience, do these lines grab your attention?

Absolutely *not*! They are too ordinary!

An audience remembers what they hear first. So you have the perfect opportunity to make something really meaningful stick.

Let's watch the first 30 seconds of one of my favorite speeches. Listen from 1:30–2:05.

https://youtu.be/Ch4Ddto7rd0

Welcome back.

That was Bill Clinton's speech at the 2016 Democratic National Convention to support his wife, Hillary.

"In the Spring of 1971, I met a girl."

He jumped right into his story.

And he took exactly seven seconds to say the first line of his speech, followed by the description of "the girl" – detailed yet succinct enough that you could almost see the young version of Hilary right away.

I didn't teach the 7–30 rule to Bill Clinton, but most excellent public speakers practice this rule in action.

If you are presenting to a global audience, and wondering, "Shouldn't I feel out the audience first and open my speech safely, because you never know what kind of reactions you'll get from a culturally diverse audience?", I understand where you're coming from.

However, what you think is safe and polite may not be so in the eye of a different culture. I call it "unpleasant pleasantry." Your intention might be to be polite by first thanking the audience, sponsor, and event organizer, or be humble by praising preceding speakers or putting yourself down by saying something like "How do I follow this amazing speaker?!," you may be sending a wrong message – that you are not a competent speaker.

Remember, in a cross-cultural situation, your common sense may not be so common.

You need a *bang!* from the get-go so that you can grab everyone's attention – no matter what culture they are from.

Now it's your turn.

You will receive the following six of my favorite powerful opening techniques that captivate your audience from the get-go.

1. Open with a story

The first, and my most favorite, technique is to start with a story.

Stories have a power to connect with the audience at the deepest level. People resist sales presentations, but no one can resist a good story . . . well told.

One thing you *don't* want to do when telling a story is to start like this:

"I'd like to tell you a story where I realized . . . ."

Why not?

Because half of your most important first seven seconds is spoiled!

Dive right into the story, just like Bill Clinton did.

Also keep in mind that your audience needs to hear a concise, well-organized story in order to remember it. Make a clear point by telling a story. Choose the story that best serves the audience. Make your story relatable.

If you want to learn more about how to craft a captivating story, make sure you enroll in my e-learning program, "The Art of Persuasive Speaking in Global Business" (https://natsuyolipschutz.us/elearning/).

2. Surprise with a fact

The second effective way to open your speech is to state a little-known fact, or some interesting statistics.

How can you bring surprise to your audience?

When you create a curiosity gap by stating a little-known fact or by sharing statistics that are directly related to your topic, you can entice the audience to say, "tell me more."

A celebrity chef, Jamie Oliver, used this opening technique in his TEDx Talk.

(https://youtu.be/BCM2PZ-SFTk?si=CaW0QgyAFt8oXWt7)

Sadly, in the next 18 minutes when I do our chat, four Americans that are alive will be dead from the food that they eat.

What? It's a shocking statistic, isn't it?

When we are shocked with a little-known fact, it opens our hearts and ears and . . . mouth . . . .

It immediately grabs our attention!

3. Rhetorical question

Here is the third way to open your speech, and one which I often use. It is to ask a rhetorical question.

If your life were a book and you were the author, how would you want your story to go? That's the question that changed my life forever.

This is the opening of Amy Purdy's speech called "Living Beyond Limits":

(https://www.ted.com/talks/amy_purdy_living_beyond_limits)

You may know Amy from Season 18 of *Dancing with the Stars*.

In case you don't know her, she is a motivational speaker, author, model, snowboarder, and double amputee. She is a two-time Paralympic medalist.

Her opening not only captures the attention of the audience immediately, but it also makes them think, because it's not just some random question.

It's a powerful question that takes the audience right into their own minds. And it's a rhetorical question, so you are not looking for the actual response or answer from the audience.

The purpose of a rhetorical question is to invite the audience to taste the flavor of the entire speech.

A few other rhetorical question examples are:

"If I were to ask you . . . ."
"What would the world be like without . . . ."
"If you had a mighty power that meant you would never fail, what would you dare to do?"

4. Let them imagine

The fourth technique you can use to grab their attention is to start with the word, "Imagine":

https://www.ted.com/talks/ric_elias_3_things_i_learned_while_my_plane_crashed

Ric Elias had a front-row seat on Flight 1549, the plane that crash-landed in the Hudson River in New York in January 2009.

He opened his TEDx Talk with these lines:

> Imagine a big explosion as you climb through 3,000 feet. Imagine a plane full of smoke. Imagine an engine going clack, clack, clack. It sounds scary. Well, I had a unique seat that day. I was sitting in 1D. I was the only one who could talk to the flight attendants.

The word "imagine" takes your audience right to the scene.

As the speaker re-lives that scene, the audience will also experience the journey together.

Also take notice that his first line took seven seconds, and he clearly painted the picture in the first 30 seconds.

The 7–30 rule.

5. Relate to their situation

The fifth tip you can use on any speaking occasion is to relate to the personal situation of your audience.

At the 2020 Democratic National Convention, former First Lady Michelle Obama opened her speech like this.[2]

> It's a hard time, and everyone's feeling it in different ways. And I know a lot of folks are reluctant to tune into a political convention right now or to politics in general. Believe me, I get that.

Every powerful speech has a "You-Focused" message.

So why don't we start with a "You-Focused" opening?

When you relate to the audience's situation from the get-go, they will immediately connect with you and feel, "This person gets me."

You can also tap into their brain and voice to explore what they may be thinking, especially when you suspect that they may have a resistance to your idea.

You could say:

"You may be thinking . . . ."

"I understand some of you may not agree with me."

In fact, Michelle Obama, in her same speech, used this tactic too.
She said:

> "I understand that my message won't be heard by some people. We live in a nation that is deeply divided, and I am a Black woman speaking at the Democratic Convention."

By addressing her opponents, she is including everyone in her world, because she is relating to all of their situations.

6. Powerful quotation

Finally, the sixth way to show your creativity is to use a powerful quotation.
This is a creative way to open your speech.
What memorable quote or saying can you use to illustrate the point you are going to make?
For example, General Eisenhower said:

> "Leadership is the ability to decide what has to be done and then to get people to want to do it."

If you are giving a leadership talk, you might start with this quote.
This is one of my favorites: Patricia Fripp's opening.
She is a hall of fame professional speaker. And in one of her keynotes, she says:

As the great philosopher Raquel Welch said, "Style is being yourself, but on purpose." Every time you stand up to address an audience, you have to be yourself, but slightly larger than life. In other words, on purpose.

It's a relevant and compelling quote, yet it is not overused – *and* she embedded humor by saying "the great philosopher Raquel Welch."
If you don't know who Raquel Welch, she was an American actress and singer, and a sex symbol in the 1960s.
Now do you get the joke?
Quotes don't have to come from famous people.
They may come from your own sources, like your parents, grandparents, children, teacher, boss, clients – you name it.

Don't bore your audience with familiar and tired quotes.
Be creative.

Now, it's your turn.
You have six options to choose from.
Choose one that will smoothly transition into the next part of your presentation.
Think about a couple of different ways to open your speech.
Write down the first four sentences of your potential opening.

Recency effect and six ways to close your presentation with a lasting impression

Your audience members will remember best what they hear first, and also, what they hear last.
This is called "the recency effect."
The recency effect is the tendency to remember the most recently presented information best.
For example, if you are trying to memorize a list of items, the recency effect means you are more likely to recall the items from the list that you studied last.
The same principle applies to your presentation.
Your last words linger, so give your closing words extra consideration.
Following are some pitfalls most speakers fall into:

Never, ever, close your presentation with, "I'm out of time," even if you are. You will then waste your final opportunity to reinforce your One BIG Message.

Also, do not close on a Q&A (question and answer period), just in case you're asked an awkward question or in case an audience member shares a rambling opinion. If you end your presentation with a Q&A, you are risking distracting questions which may diminish your impact on your audience. Especially with a culturally diverse audience, you never know what unexpected questions you may receive.

You can thank your audience for the opportunity to speak, but don't make these your last words. Instead, close your speech with words that support your presentation and maximize your impact.
Remember the recency effect. Last words linger. This will determine how your audience feels once they walk out of the doors and go back to their lives.
You can give a wonderful speech – but if the ending is weak, your audience will walk away feeling like the speech wasn't very strong.

Closing your speech with impact can open up doors of opportunities. So here are six of my favorite tips for you to consider using to create a powerful closing.

1. Call to action

First and foremost, create a call to action.

Good speakers give speeches that get a good response, but great speakers give speeches that move their audience to take action. Great speakers help change lives long after they have finished speaking.

The one common purpose for every single presentation – no matter what kind or what length – is to make your audience think, feel, and act differently after you have spoken.

Especially in business, you want this presentation to open up a door of opportunity or lead to the next step . . . it may be a meeting with the decision maker; it may be that you want the audience to register for your next event; it may be that you hope they will submit a quote to you.

Think about the exact next step you expect them to take.

Clearly state that one next step in your closing.

Again, just one.

If you give them a few options, they will be confused and will most likely *not* take *any* action at all.

In order to inspire your audience to take action, they need to clearly see the benefit of taking this particular step you are suggesting.

You can compare and contrast between now and the future, what they don't want compared to what they do. Describe their life without taking an action based on your idea, and then describe their life with.

When they are able to see a big enhancement, it's a no-brainer.

After you have used the compare and contrast technique to build up to the grand finale, make sure you end on a high note.

Brian Tracy, a world-renowned speaker, consultant, and author, often uses this technique.

I had the pleasure of co-authoring with him a book called *The Success Blueprint*.

Brian Tracy says, in business, always end a speech with a call to action.

For example:

We have great challenges and great opportunities, and with your help, we will meet them and make this next year the best year in our history!

Say your closing line with strength and determination, and drive your One BIG Message home.

You may also say one of the following:

"Your next step is . . . ."
"I challenge you to . . . ."
"When will you . . . ."
"How will you . . . ."

Your audience will surely be motivated to take action.

2. Circular method

Second, circle back to the opening.

Before you are settled with your closing, go back to the beginning and review how you opened, so you can determine if there's an opportunity to tie it in.

When you close your presentation with the same words, thoughts, or story from your opening, it is called the circular approach, and it's like tying a bow around your message.

If you opened with a story, don't finish telling the whole story in your opening. Leave the conclusion to the closing. This suspense will give your audience a tease and they will want to know how your story ends. If you opened with a question, you can ask another question to make sure their answer will be aligned with your points. This will help your audience focus again on your One BIG Message.

You could open with a statement, and bookend your speech with the same statement, like Brené Brown did at the virtual commencement at the University of Texas in 2020.

She opened her speech with this statement:

I believe that what starts at University of Texas changes the world . . .
What starts here changes the world, but it will not be on your terms, and it will not be on your timeline.[3]

In closing, she said:

It will not be on your terms or on your timeline. The world does not ready itself for our plans. But make no mistake. What starts at the University of Texas changes the world.[4]

Think about how you can tie your closing into your opening.

Remember, your last words linger. Leave them with a reinforcement of a key idea or an inspirational thought from your presentation.

3. Relevant quotation

Third, a relevant quotation.

Is there a quotation you can use to sum up your message in a memorable way? It has to align with your message. Be intentional about selecting a quotation. Your goal is to be remembered and repeated. This is not a time to add a new idea.

One of my clients, who is a serial entrepreneur and currently a co-founder of a flying car company, closed her speech with a Thomas Edison quotation.

You might have heard his famous quote,

"I have not failed. I've just found 10,000 ways that won't work."

As an entrepreneur, this quote would have been good, too.

But this is overquoted by many, and my client thought another quote from Thomas Edison would better align with her message.

Her core message was, "never give up."

So we chose this quote:

> Our greatest weakness lies in giving up. The most certain way to succeed is always to try just one more time.

Again, be intentional about selecting a relevant quotation. Find something that's not overused, yet still resonates with the audience.

4. Powerful question

Fourth, a powerful question.

Nothing has such power to cause a mental shift as that of a question.

It is true in our conversations, our meetings, and also in our presentations.

Questions spark curiosity, increase motivation, pose a challenge, or generate deep thoughts.

Your last words linger. Leave your audience to ponder.

When you close with a powerful question that captures your message and directly ties into your call for action, it will leave the audience thinking more deeply – and ultimately then be more inclined to take action.

You could also use a circular approach by setting up a question at the opening of your speech, asking the same question again, and using your closing to answer it. But when your presentation is clear and complete, just asking a powerful question is memorable enough. Because their mental shift has already occurred during your presentation, and they will already know the answer.

When British actor Emma Watson gave a speech on gender equality at the 2014 United Nations assembly, she closed her speech with a powerful question:

> If you believe in equality, you might be one of those inadvertent feminists that I spoke of earlier, and for this, I applaud you. We are struggling for a uniting word, but the good news is, we have a uniting movement. It is called HeForShe. I invite you to step forward, to be seen and to ask yourself, "If not me, who? If not now, when?"[5]

5. Personal story

Fifth, your personal story.

Stories are a great way for you to teach and train, inspire and motivate, inform and educate. You can simplify a complex idea, demonstrate value, and make principles more concrete.

A powerful closing story could provide your audience with hope and proof that your message will work for them.

Jack Ma, the founder and chairman of the e-commerce giant Alibaba, gave a talk at the 2017 World Economic Forum.

He told his personal story that he had been rejected time after time by multiple organizations, including Harvard University. His One BIG Message in this talk was "Never give up."

He ended his talk with a brief story of Forrest Gump.

He said:

> We are like Forrest Gump. This guy has hope. Like Forrest Gump, we keep on fighting. We keep on changing ourselves. We don't complain. We should never give up.[6]

One tip about storytelling.

Stories are always about people. Give your character a name.

If you can't use their real names, you can say, "let's call him Joe." "Joe" could be "Joanne." It doesn't matter. People have a backstory, their title or years of experience, and your audience want to hear what your characters look like and sound like, what they think or say, how they feel or act. Give your character a life.

My clients often ask me, "If I tell my whole story, it'll be way too long. Does my story have to be 100% accurate?"

Stories have to be true. But they do not have to be 100% accurate. Stories should shrink time to make your point.

Be clear. What is the Main Point you want to reinforce through your story?

6. Let them say it

Sixth, let them say it.

You want to close your presentation with words that support your message and maximize your impact.

It is a good idea to use closing to review your Main Points.

It is an even better idea to let the audience verbalize your points.

Of course, it is crucial that you have been building up to your points and reinforcing memorable short phrases, so your audience can recall, repeat, and relate.

How can you get them to verbalize your points?

Well, in case of my keynote, I talk about the 3-Step Process of effective cross-cultural communications.

To anchor my message, I use an acronym – the 3As: Acknowledge, Analyze, and Adapt.

And every time I go through a point, I repeat these 3As. By the end of my keynote, my audience has learned the 3As by heart. They are ready to call them out.

When I use this technique, I would start by saying, "Today, we explored the 3-Step Process called the 3As. The first A is . . . ?"

I would also add in a hand gesture to invite them to say it out loud.

The key to successfully letting them say it is this simple formula:

Explain to them what you are going to tell them. Give them the key information. Then recap what you've told them.

When they hear it repeatedly, they'll memorize it.

When they vocalize it, they'll internalize it.

Now, it's your turn.

You have six options to choose from.

Think about a couple of different ways to powerfully end your speech with a lasting impression.

Write down the last four sentences of your potential closing.

Now you have learned everything you need to give a persuasive presentation to your global audience.

I will leave you with six practical tips you want to remember when presenting persuasively to a global audience.

1. Focus on your One BIG Message

I once coached a group of very experienced senior leaders to deliver a presentation at their internal leadership conference with all the global locations.

The audience was all senior executives and they each had 10 minutes to present on the direction of their teams for the next two years.

It was clear to me why these individuals were leaders of very high-performing teams. They had clear visions. They knew their business strategy inside out. They had specific action plans to achieve their two-year goals. Each one could describe in detail their teams' strengths, the results they'd achieved in the last few years, and the lessons learned – so encapsulating it all in a presentation seemed simple, right?!

Yet as I listened to each of their presentations, there was nothing about them that was in the least bit memorable. In fact, despite the impressive facts and figures that they reeled off, they were starting to sound a little repetitive and – dare I say it? – boring.

What were they missing?

It was the fact that they had no core message – no One BIG Message. The *one* thing that they wanted their audience to remember and take action on was missing.

You have noticed by now how I've been repeating the importance of One BIG Message, right? And I cannot emphasize enough how important it is. If you want your presentation to be persuasive and memorable even through culturally diverse lenses, you must present your One BIG Message again, and again, and again, throughout our presentation consistently, so that your message will not be interpreted in different ways.

2. Does your One BIG Message describe your presentation?

Everything about your presentation should be around your One BIG Message: the story you tell, the facts you present, the graphics and graphs you show, your slides (if you have them), the transition, the intro, and the closing.

You may be hung up on keeping some slides just because you or your team have been using all this time. But anything that doesn't relate to your One BIG Message either gets cut or is adapted to fit.

Yes, you may feel uneasy. Yes, it takes courage. But think about how diamonds are made.

Diamonds are found in rough rock formations. Chiseling and cutting are vital to reveal their beauty. This process removes surface imperfections, reveals internal inclusions, and maximizes light reflection. Polishing further refines the gem's appearance, transforming it into the brilliant, shiny diamond we know. If you think, "Oh, this rock is part of the diamond. What a waste. Maybe I won't chisel it off but keep the whole rock. I know there is value in it," no one will see the value. Right? Refining your One BIG Message goes the same way. Treat your message as if you are polishing a rock into a shiny diamond.

Your key points to support One BIG Message should flow logically from one to another, for example: 1) this is the problem, 2) these are the possible solutions, and 3) this is what we're going to do.

Business presentations are crucial not only to impart knowledge and share crucial information but also to help your audience grow and develop.

If your presentation is hard to follow, or if your argument or reasoning is not strong enough, your audience will easily dismiss your ideas. Sound, logical arguments, on the other hand, are hard for your audience to ignore.

3. Eliminate absolute terms

Think about how you would feel if you heard me say:

"This is the best iPhone to use because it has a long battery life."

For them, the best phone may be another model with better camera. Or it could be the one with better connectivity.

But with this argument, I'm leaving out "You-Focused perspectives" – your point of view. As a result, my argument sounds not persuasive enough for them.

We want to be careful about using absolute terms, like "best," "only," "always," "everyone," "perfect." People's perceptions are different. So absolute terms could also compromise logic.

Just because something has a factual claim, doesn't mean it will "always" connect with your audience.

What if I improved my argument and said:

> "When you're dashing from meeting to meeting and always on the go, you need an iPhone that has a long battery life so you don't lose connection with the people that matter the most."

Do you see the difference?

I've related my facts to my audience because I know they are busy people who don't have time to charge their phones several times in a day.

I've set up a situation that they can relate to, and now they're interested in what I have to say.

The key here is to have a clear understanding of your audience, because without that, you will lack the connection to the logic.

4. Is it repeatable?

Make sure that your core message is repeatable. In other words, when you've described it in one sentence, is it easy and succinct for others to repeat it?

Try it on your colleague, wife, husband, partner, or child tonight and see if they can repeat it as well as you – with no help! That's why your One BIG Message needs to be ten words or fewer.

5. Is it relatable to my audience?

The key to having a successful One BIG Message is that it is relatable to the audience in the room.

Think about:

> Why are they attending? What are they hoping to learn/discover?
>
> Why should they care about your presentation, and what benefits could it bring to them?

The presentation is not to demonstrate how much you know about any given topic. It's what you can impart specifically to them to help them learn, grow, and develop.

6. Start at the end

When I'm coaching very senior executives, I like to start with the end goal.

What do you want your audience to think/feel/do at the end of your presentation?

Make it ONE thing that you want your audience to take action on.

Write it down in a sentence and then say it out loud to see if it sounds convincing.

Remember that presentations are an iterative process, so be prepared for several versions before you agree on the winning message.

Now you are ready to take the stage, present, and captivate your global audience.

Let me know if you need more fine-tuning. It is always (here I'm deliberately using an absolute term!!) a good idea to get professional advice to get to where you want to go, faster.

Notes

1 Syd Field, *Screenplay: The Foundations of Screenwriting*, rev. ed. (New York: Delta, 2005).
2 Michelle Obama, "Michelle Obama's DNC speech," PBS NewsHour, August 17, 2020, YouTube video, 18:31, 8:53–9:14, https://www.youtube.com/watch?v=uKy3iiWjhVI.
3 Brené Brown, "Don't Be Afraid to Fall: Brené Brown Addresses the University of Texas at Austin's 2020 Graduates," The University of Texas at Austin, May 24, 2020, YouTube video, 21:07, 1:38–1:47, https://youtu.be/wMV77xYdEa4?si=UCaFTMIy_ZfsyGzj.
4 Brené Brown, "Don't Be Afraid to Fall: Brené Brown Addresses the University of Texas at Austin's 2020 Graduates," The University of Texas at Austin, May 24, 2020, YouTube video, 21:07, 20:26–20:44, https://youtu.be/wMV77xYdEa4?si=UCaFTMIy_ZfsyGzj.
5 Emma Watson, "Emma Watson at the HeforShe Campaign 2014," United Nations, September 22, 2014, YouTube video, from YouTube courtesy of United Nations, September 22, 2014, video, 13:15, 11:48–12:26, https://youtu.be/gkjW9PZBRfk?si=Z4gfp6wuA2RrgVFt.
6 Jack Ma, "Jack Ma: I've Had Lots of Failures and Rejections," World Economic Forum, February 3, 2015, YouTube video, 44:32, 43:49–44:17, https://youtu.be/1O3ghiyirvU?si=bjobzF18fA4qbj0R.

Chapter 4

Communicate to transform your global team from good to great

A few years ago, I gave a three-day facilitated workshop at the annual executive conference of a leading Japanese electronics company in the U.S. Let's call it "H Corp."

Twenty-five senior members representing various departments and locations in North America had gathered at their New Jersey headquarters. Those 25 participants had origins from around the world: Japan, the United States, Korea, China, India, Columbia, France, Canada, Mexico, and Russia. Some directly worked together; others barely knew each other.

The main purpose of these facilitated sessions was to: 1) clarify and deepen understanding of H Corp's three-year strategy, and 2) develop specific action plans for each of their locations.

* * *

Day 1.

The president of H Corp, Mr. Ozaki, gives a short presentation on the three-year strategy, and his expectations for all participants.

"At the end of this three-day workshop, I need to see actionable plans from all of you. Let's bring our knowledge together! Natsuyo san will guide us through."

Mr. Ozaki gestures to me to begin.

I start with an energizing ice-breaking activity called "Paper Tower."

The task is simple. Build the tallest tower using only paper.

Participants are grouped into pre-assigned groups of five.

Among the participants are some people who don't usually interact with each other, so they are uptight at first. This ice-breaking activity is designed to help them engage freely and have open dialogue.

I give clear instructions:

In your group, take seven minutes to discuss the Paper Tower building strategy. During this discussion time, you may use only one sheet of

DOI: 10.4324/9781003455615-5

paper. You can fold or tear paper by hand, but no tools are allowed. The tower has to stand by itself without any support for 10 seconds. The group that builds the tallest tower wins.

After the discussion time, you have 45 seconds to build a tower.

Any questions?

OK, seven minutes of discussion time starts . . . *now*!

President Ozaki and I observe the group discussion.

In Group 1, R&D director Choi, engineering manager Raj, and sales director Kitano were actively taking turns to lead the discussion. Kitano suggests an overall shape of the tower, Raj provides structural tips, and Choi experiments with a sheet of paper.

Group 2 is rather quiet. Plant manager Pablo starts folding the paper into a long triangular cylinder, as accounting manager Yuko and sales manager Carol observe him.

"That may be a bit wobbly. What about this shape?" HR manager Wang folds the paper like an accordion.

"Hmm, that's interesting. But that may be difficult to stack. What if I fold it like a square?" Carol says. Then there is an uncomfortable silence.

Participants in Group 3 are constantly laughing and joking with each other.

"You guys are really having fun!" President Ozaki says, and laughs, too.

Discussion in Group 4 is being led by vice president Tajima.

"That's a great idea, Roy! What do you guys think? Any other ideas?" Others contribute their ideas, then Tajima assigns paper folders and builders, and he volunteers to be a timer.

Group 5 is getting louder. I walk over there, as Chief Engineer Vladmir is giving his speech about the importance of building a strong foundation. He shows how exactly the paper should be folded. A branch director, Francois, interjects and claims that Vladmir's way would take too much time, and suggests they focus on making the tower tall, not precise.

"No! Then the tower will collapse! If we spend the time to build a solid first layer, stacking up becomes easier and faster!" Vladmir insists.

"Well, the tower only has to stand for 10 seconds, right? If it collapses after 10 seconds, it doesn't matter! We still win!" Francois counters.

While Vladmir and Francois continue arguing, other members seem disconnected.

"One more minute!!" I shout out, and start counting down. Sixty seconds later I declare: "Time is up! Now clear the table, get ready to build. Forty-five seconds. Get set, go!"

All groups get quiet. The rustling sound of paper permeates the room.

"10 seconds!"

"Oh my gosh!!!" "What?!?!" "Oh no!!!!" "One more, one more!!"
Quiet turns to near-panic.
"3–2–1, hands off!!!!"
I hear a mix of deep sighs, screams, relieved voices, and laughs.

Group 1 and Group 4 tie with four levels. Group 2 is the first runner up with three levels. Group 3 had a very interesting looking one-story tower. Group 5 had a very wide bottom and a vertically placed triangular cylinder on top.

"Let's debrief."

"Group 1 and Group 4, what do you think you did well?"

Roy in Group 4 speaks up first.

"Tajima san asked questions, listened to our ideas, and delegated tasks. So it was efficient. We were also aware of how short 45 seconds would be."

Choi in Group 1 says,

"In our Group, we used our own specialized knowledge and equally contributed."

Raj adds, "And we also aimed for four levels, and we did just that."

"I see. So Group 4 had one person who guided the whole discussion process, as well as the actual building process within 45 seconds. And people in Group 1 knew their own roles and visualized the goal. Correct?"

I quickly summarize what I just heard.

"And . . . what happened to Group 3?"

Everyone laughs as they look at a one-story tower with different shapes and heights of paper all over the place.

I turn to Group 5 and ask, "What about this group? If you had another chance, what would you do differently?"

Before Vladmir opens his mouth, Francois raises his hand and says, "Well, we couldn't come to an agreement even with one minute left, so we just went with Vladmir's idea without a plan."

Vladmir shrugs his shoulders with raised arms and flat hands.

"Every group had different team dynamics, and very different approaches. Interesting."

I leave my comment at that, and everyone nods in agreement.

For the first time since the beginning of the session, I turn on the slide.

"Let's think about key elements a team needs to perform well together."

Group vs. team

"When we just debriefed, I purposefully used the word, 'group' instead of 'team.' What do you think is the difference between a 'group' and a 'team'?"

I pose a question to kick off the content of the workshop.

I alternate an interactive lecture and group discussion as I conduct the workshop.

It went like this. Imagine yourself as if you are sitting in this workshop with H Corp.

* * *

The terms "group" and "team" are often used interchangeably, but they have distinct characteristics that differentiate them.

A group is a collection of individuals who are brought together for a common purpose or objective. However, each individual works independently to achieve their goals, and the group's purpose may not be interdependent. So the result of a group is a mere sum of the individuals.

A team is a group of people with complementary skills and abilities, working collaboratively toward a shared objective or goal. The achievement of the goal is interdependent, meaning each member's efforts are crucial for success. Therefore, the result of a team is a multiplier. They produce synergy.

A group

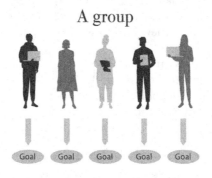

A team

Differences between a group and a team

For example, accountability is shared among team members. They hold each other responsible for their contributions and the overall success of the team.

Group 4 demonstrated this attribute, thanks to Tajima's facilitative communication style.

Team members also rely on each other's contributions, skills, and efforts to achieve a common goal. The success of one team member is tied to the success of the entire team. Their roles were also clear and complement each other. Group 1 demonstrated this.

So a team is a specialized form of a group whereby members collaborate interdependently and produce more than they can alone, because they share a common understanding of goal directions, clear roles, and effective communication.

Three elements of a high-performance team

In order to become a high-performance team, however, you must establish three crucial elements in your team: Alignment, Process, and People.

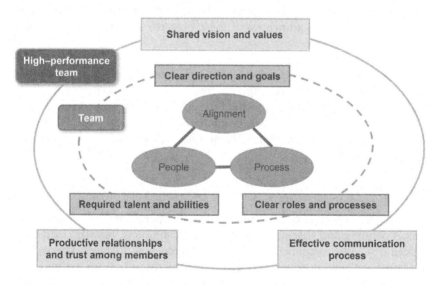

What it takes to become a high-performance team

1. Alignment

First and foremost, each member of a team must share clear objectives and strategies, so that their personal goals and company or team goals are aligned.

Throughout my strategy consulting career, I've seen many companies lacking alignment.

Following are three most common cases where alignment is lacking in the team:

- Vague objectives: For instance, having a slogan like "Global Growth!" without specifying when, in which areas, and to what extent the growth should occur, would leave the team members unsure of where they need to go and what their responsibilities are.
- Lack of specificity in strategy: Simply stating a goal like "Double global sales in three years" without clear strategies and guidelines for achieving it results in an ambiguous approach. Effective strategies may involve specifying how to conquer certain regions or strengthen technological capabilities through specific measures.
- Insufficient communication: Objectives and strategies might be communicated once at the beginning of the fiscal year, or through one-way communication. But this would be a guaranteed failure. Insufficient communication leaves questions about how well members understand the team's objectives and strategies. Team members may secretly harbor doubts about the significance of these objectives or whether achieving them is even feasible.

To ensure improved productivity of a global team and to bring a good team to a high-performance team, it is imperative to align each team member's directions by: 1) defining what the team aims to achieve (objectives), 2) clarifying what aspects are emphasized (strategies), and 3) ensuring that everyone comprehends the significance of these objectives and strategies.

2. Process

Next, it is crucial to establish the team's operational processes. This entails defining and sharing the way the team conducts its work, including procedures, role assignments, rules, and agreements. In cases where clear processes are lacking or not properly shared within the team, redundancy and omissions can occur, leading to inefficiency, confusion, and poor productivity. In such cases, the team cannot perform well or create synergy, but remains as a mere collection of individuals – a "group" rather than a "team."

When working in a single-culture team, it might be possible for team members to "read between the lines" and understand the essential points and how to proceed without explicitly expressing processes, because there are implicitly shared values and the ability to complement each other's roles seamlessly. This is often seen in the "High Context culture." However, in global teams, it is essential to presume that such mutual understanding cannot be taken for granted. Clearly defining processes and ensuring their thorough communication (Low Context) becomes crucial. It's not only about defining each member's role and determining the basic PDCA (Plan–Do–Check–Act) cycle for the team, but also specifying approaches for issue resolution should problems arise.

3. People

The "people" aspect involves constituting the team with members possessing the skills and abilities necessary to achieve the team's objectives. In a High Context culture, it's not uncommon to gather team members first and then assess their skills and abilities. The tasks assigned and the volume of work might be adjusted accordingly. There is the premise that no matter which individuals are placed on the team, the variation in skills, abilities, and values will fall within a reasonably expected range.

However, when operating global teams, it is essential to clearly define what skills and abilities are needed to achieve the team's objectives. Additionally, planning how to address any skills or abilities that might be lacking and ensuring individual growth should also be considered in advance.

Global teams often comprise members with diverse backgrounds. To effectively manage teams with increased diversity, these three elements – Alignment, Process, and People – are indispensable.

Then, the big question is: What skills and leadership styles are required to develop, maintain, and lead a high-performance team?

Leadership styles

Leadership was once believed to be innate, but I strongly believe that it's earned through daily efforts and experiences. Leaders are nurtured, not born naturally.

Becoming a leader doesn't necessarily mean becoming the head of an organization. It's about sticking to what you believe is right and passionate about, and most importantly, influencing others in a positive way.

But there are multiple styles of leadership, and effective leaders can adapt their leadership styles depending on situations, motivation level, or skill level of their team members.

Based on my years of working with global companies, I categorized them into three styles. Let's explore.

1. Visionary leader: leading from the front

These are the "achievement-oriented" leaders who courageously pursue high goals and passions, and foresee future developments based on worldly trends. They are usually powerful, and people tend to be inspired and follow their lead.

2. Catalyst leader: facilitating within

These leaders gather capable and diverse individuals, encouraging collaborative efforts among them, and bringing out each individual's strengths to create synergy. People are drawn to these leaders because they create an environment where a team can generate more than their individual capacities combined.

3. Servant leader: serving from behind

These leaders support individuals from behind, ensuring they can perform at their best and supporting them only when necessary. This style is often seen in long-established teams.

What's important for us to understand here is that no one style is better than another. Since leadership is rooted in one's inherent qualities, there's no fixed template, and it's situational.

In fact, teams are never stagnant. They always evolve, and leaders must be able to Adapt their leadership styles depending on what stage their teams are in at that point.

If I dare choose the single most important skill for global leaders to hone to Adapt, it would be facilitation skills. Whether your natural leadership style is "visionary" or "catalyst" or "servant," facilitation skills are critical to navigating your team through various development stages.

Before we go deep dive into facilitation skills, it's important for us to understand the team development stages. Let's explore.

Team development stages

When working with a diverse team, team dynamics always evolve. As a global leader aiming to transform your diverse team to a high-performance team, you need to understand the stages of team development and facilitate your team accordingly.

According to Bruce Tuckman,[1] a team goes through the following five stages.

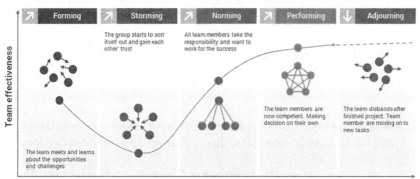

Tuckman's Team Development Stages

Forming stage

Team members are introduced, and they try to figure out their roles and responsibilities. It's a phase of orientation and anticipation. This often occurs when a new team is assembled for a specific project.

Storming stage

When they start to get to know each other, individuals start expressing their opinions and ideas. It's a clash of perspectives, much like a brainstorming session when various ideas are debated and challenged. In business, this can be a stage of creative conflict whereby differing strategies are discussed passionately.

Norming stage

The team starts to settle into defined roles and norms. Agreement is reached on how the team will operate, and consensus is built around goals and expectations. This phase is marked by a sense of unity and cooperation within the team. Business-wise, it's when everyone is on the same page and working harmoniously toward shared objectives.

Performing stage

The performing stage is when the team is functioning at its peak. Each member knows their role and works efficiently toward the team's objectives. There's a high level of trust, and tasks are executed with excellence. It's the stage when productivity is at its best, and accomplishments are notable.

Adjourning (or transforming)

The project or task is completed successfully. If the team achieved its goals, there's a sense of accomplishment and celebration. On the other hand, if the project is ongoing or the team is transitioning to a new task, it's a transformation phase. This could involve reorganizing the team, integrating lessons learned, and gearing up for the next endeavor.

It's important to note that teams aren't rigidly confined to one stage at a time. They can move back and forth, especially when new members join or circumstances change. Facilitative leadership and communication strategy play pivotal roles in helping the team progress smoothly through these stages.

However. "Smooth" does *not* mean rushing through or skipping the storming stage.

In a culturally diverse team, for instance, you will observe different reactions in the storming stage. People from Low Context cultures with individualism and uncertainty avoidance tendencies may be more immune to conflict. "I like you but I don't like your opinion" is accepted, and they are willing to openly discuss their differences.

However, High Context people may see it as a conflict they want to avoid, as they tend to think "If I like you, I won't openly be opposed to your idea," or "I don't like you; therefore, I don't like your opinion." They tend to put the "person" and the "act" or "thoughts" into one basket. There is a Japanese saying, "When you despise a monk, you even hate his Buddhist robe."

But if this were to be translated into a Low Context way, it would be "Hate the sin, love the sinner." See the separation between the person and the act?

Harmony is the priority for people from High Context culture with collectivism and uncertainty avoidance high tendencies. They don't like conflicts. They would use every power to avoid conflict, and skip through the storming stage, often resulting in superficial conversations. However, if they feel that the relationship, respect, and harmony are neglected, they may quietly resist, causing a silent storming stage.

So it is crucial for a global facilitator to carefully navigate through the storming stage. If discussions seem to be superficial or shallow, a skilled facilitator may provoke members to intentionally cause the storming stage. If the discussion is too intense, a facilitator may ease the intensity and help the team focus on productive discussions and move forward.

Moreover, during the storming stage, team members often experience conflicts, disagreements, and challenges in defining their roles and processes. Facilitation skills can make all the difference. Here are some other elements to look out for in this stage:

Conflict resolution and understanding: During the storming stage, conflicts often arise due to differences in communication styles, cultural norms, or work approaches. Effective facilitation helps in understanding these differences, addressing conflicts constructively, and finding solutions that accommodate various viewpoints.

Cultural sensitivity and awareness: Global teams comprise individuals with diverse cultural backgrounds. The storming stage provides an opportunity to increase cultural sensitivity and awareness of these differences. A team leader must act as a bridge. Effective facilitation fosters an environment whereby team members appreciate diverse perspectives and learn to collaborate across cultures.

Alignment and goal clarity: Facilitating storming helps in clarifying team goals, roles, and expectations. This alignment is crucial for a global team, as it ensures that despite geographical dispersion, everyone is on the same page regarding the team's objectives and their individual contributions.

Building trust and cohesion: Trust is fundamental for any successful team, and yet while it takes a long time to build trust, it is so easy to get lost. The storming stage often challenges trust due to conflicts. Effective facilitation encourages open communication, active listening, and empathy, building trust among team members. Cohesion is fostered when conflicts are addressed, and a sense of unity is established.

Enhanced communication: Effective facilitation promotes improved communication strategies within the team. It encourages the expression of ideas, concerns, and feedback, leading to a better understanding of each other's perspectives. In a global team, where communication can be a significant challenge, this is particularly important.

Conflict to consensus into creativity

Conflict, when managed well, can be transformed into consensus, and even fuel creativity and innovation. Effective facilitation can transform negative conflicts into productive discussions, enabling the team to generate creative solutions and approaches to tasks or challenges.

Long-term performance

Successfully navigating the storming stage leads to a more resilient team, and smooth transition to the norming and performing stages. Once conflicts are addressed and processes are refined, the team is better equipped to work together effectively in the norming and performing stages, ultimately enhancing overall team performance and productivity.

Retention and employee satisfaction

Addressing conflicts and fostering a positive team environment increases employee satisfaction and retention. When team members feel heard, valued, and part of a cohesive team, they are more likely to remain committed and engaged.

Effectively facilitating the storming stage in a global team is about managing conflicts, promoting understanding, and building a strong foundation for collaboration. It contributes to improved communication, increased productivity, and a more harmonious and successful global team.

Facilitation skills are the single most critical skills in nurturing a high-performance team in a global environment, as they enable leaders to connect with their team members, understand their needs, align team members' goals with corporate goals, close cultural gaps, and foster a collaborative and inclusive team environment.

What does a global facilitative leader do?

In order to develop a high-performance team in a global environment, effective global facilitative leaders *do not*:

- Dominate the conversation
- Order team members to conduct a task
- Provide solutions
- Give opinions or advice
- Criticize or undermine different opinions

But rather, they *do*:

> - Take a neutral position
> - Manage the problem-solving and communication process of the team
> - Support the team to maximize results
> - Act as a cultural bridge and help interpret globally diverse behaviors
> - Help create synergy of team efforts and build momentum to accomplish team tasks

When a global team has such a facilitative leader, the team can benefit in the following ways.

> - Team members can concentrate on the discussion itself, without worrying about the process or time-keeping
> - Team members are better able to consider, discuss, make decisions, and act based on the process or customer needs
> - Knowledge and wisdom of all team members will be fully utilized
> - Acts as a cultural bridge to help others adapt their style for effective communication and teamwork
> - Team will have support in problem-solving, breaking through, and decision-making
> - Team will become more close-knit and cooperative
> - Efficiency of meeting increases
> - Participants' ownership in the decision and motivation toward accomplishment of the tasks increase
> - Promotes empowerment within the organization

Five critical skills for a facilitator

So what exactly is a facilitation skill?

It's actually a collection of skills, instead of one specific skill. That's why facilitation skills are sometimes considered ambiguous.

Leading a high-performance team across diverse cultures demands a multifaceted skillset. Effective facilitation is essential in guiding and aligning team members toward common objectives while navigating cultural differences.

Let me decode these ambiguous facilitation skills by highlighting five most critical skills for an effective facilitator, and explore how they contribute to successful facilitation within culturally diverse teams.

1. Cultural intelligence

Cultural intelligence (CQ) is the bedrock of effective facilitation across cultures. It involves understanding, respecting, and adapting to diverse cultural norms, values, behaviors, and communication styles. An effective facilitator with high CQ can navigate through various cultural contexts, adjust their approach, and bridge gaps in understanding and communication. Make sure you master the cultural models we learned in the earlier chapters of this book, and always Acknowledge, Analyze, and Adapt.

The 3As you've already learned in this book allow you to recognize and respect the diverse norms, values, communication styles, and behavioral patterns present in a multicultural team. Different cultures have distinct ways of expressing opinions, handling conflict, and making decisions. Understanding these nuances is essential for effective communication and collaboration.

Being adaptable and flexible is fundamental when working with a high-performance team across cultures. Flexibility in scheduling, communication styles, and problem-solving approaches is necessary to accommodate the diverse needs and preferences of team members from different cultural backgrounds.

2. Low Context communication

Clear and direct communication is crucial to ensure that messages are conveyed accurately, especially in a multicultural environment where language proficiency may vary. Facilitators must articulate objectives, expectations, and instructions clearly, leaving no room for misinterpretation. We learned this communication style to be the "Low Context" communication style.

In a cross-cultural team, the facilitator can set clear expectations for an upcoming collaborative task. They provide a detailed explanation of the task's purpose, expected outcomes, and specific roles, ensuring that every team member comprehends their responsibilities. Do not assume they know what you know. Remember the iceberg? "What" you see or hear may not have the same "Why" – why they do what they do. You need to clearly communicate the "Why" so that everyone is on the same page.

3. Active listening

Effective communication is the cornerstone of successful facilitation. It involves not only articulating thoughts clearly but also actively listening to and understanding others. In a culturally diverse team, effective communication is even more critical due to potential language barriers, varying communication styles, and diverse interpretations.

Active listening is a vital component of effective communication. Facilitators need to listen attentively, understand perspectives, and demonstrate empathy. Acknowledging and valuing diverse viewpoints, even when they differ from the facilitator's own cultural lens, fosters an environment of openness and collaboration.

In fact, active listening is not just about listening. It involves three steps.

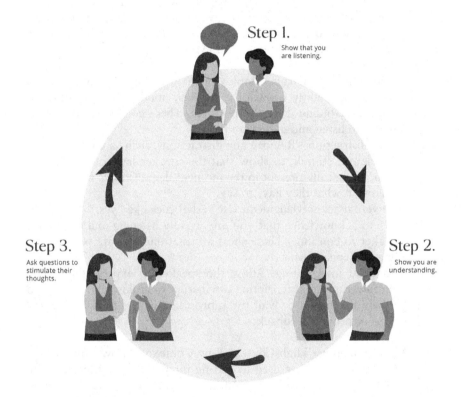

3 Steps of active listening

Step 1: show that you are listening

The first step in active listening involves demonstrating to the speaker that you are fully present and attentive to what they are saying. This step is crucial because it sets the foundation for a constructive and open conversation.

So what can you do to show the other person that you are listening? Consider the following 5 strategies:

- Maintain eye contact: Eye contact is a powerful nonverbal cue that shows you are focused and engaged. Keeping eye contact with the speaker indicates your interest and attentiveness to their words.

    However, keep in mind High Context and Low Context. For people in high context culture, intense eye contact could make them uncomfortable. Make the appropriate amount of eye contact, and sometimes intentionally look away only so slightly to give them some room. If you are talking to a Low Context person, don't be afraid to look straight into their eyes.

- Use positive body language: Employ open and inviting body language, such as leaning slightly toward the speaker, nodding your head occasionally, and avoiding defensive postures. These gestures convey your willingness to listen and understand.
- Minimize distractions: Remove any distractions, such as your phone or other irrelevant stimuli, to show that the speaker has your undivided attention. Being fully present in the moment demonstrates your respect and interest in what they have to say.
- Provide verbal acknowledgment: Use verbal cues like "yes," "I see," or "go on" to acknowledge that you are actively listening and encourage the speaker to continue. These short affirmations indicate your understanding and engagement.
- Refrain from interrupting: Allow the speaker to express themselves without interruption. Interrupting can disrupt their flow of thought and make them feel unheard. Wait for appropriate pauses to ask clarifying questions or provide feedback.

    Again, remember High Context–Low Context. A Low Context person might be more used to getting interrupted, and interruption may not discourage them from talking. However, a High Context person may lose momentum when they get interrupted.

Step 2: show that you understand

After establishing that you are attentive and engaged, the next step is to convey that you comprehend the speaker's message. Understanding goes beyond just hearing the words – it involves grasping the underlying meaning, emotions, and perspectives.

Here are five strategies you can employ:

1. Paraphrase and summarize: Repeat what the speaker has said in your own words to confirm your understanding and show empathy. Summarize the Main Points to demonstrate that you are actively processing the information.
2. Mirror emotions and feelings: Acknowledge the emotions and feelings expressed by the speaker. Reflecting their emotions back to them, such as saying "It sounds like you're feeling frustrated," validates their experiences and fosters a sense of empathy. Sometimes, simply mirroring the speaker's facial expression might suffice.
3. Validate perspectives: Even if you don't agree with the speaker's viewpoint, validate their perspective by acknowledging its legitimacy. Understanding is about acknowledging and respecting different opinions and viewpoints, not about agreeing and complying in expense for your own thoughts.
4. Empathize with the speaker: Put yourself in the speaker's shoes and imagine how they might be feeling or thinking. Expressing empathy helps the speaker feel understood and supported, creating a conducive environment for open dialogue.
5. Ask clarifying questions: Seek clarification if there's something you don't fully understand. This demonstrates your commitment to grasping the nuances of the speaker's message and ensures accurate interpretation.

Step 3: ask questions to stimulate their thoughts

The final and the most important step in active listening involves encouraging the speaker to elaborate on their thoughts and ideas by asking insightful and thought-provoking questions. These questions stimulate deeper reflection and enable a more meaningful exchange of ideas.

In fact, questioning technique is crucial in one-on-one conversations as well. We will explore this more deeply in the next chapter, but let me plant the seeds here by introducing different types of questions you can utilize.

Open-ended questions

Open-ended questions are a type of question in which their answers require more than yes or no. They are designed to prompt detailed, thoughtful responses from the respondent.

They encourage elaboration, self-reflection, and the expression of ideas, feelings, or opinions. These questions do not have a specific answer and usually begin with words like "what," "who," "why," "what," "where," "how," or "tell me more about . . . ."

Here are some examples of open-ended questions:

"Can you describe your experience at the event?"

"How do you feel about the recent changes in the workplace?"

"What are your thoughts on the new project proposal?"

"Tell me about a time when you felt truly accomplished in your work."

Open-ended questions promote deeper understanding, facilitate exploration of ideas, and invite the speaker to provide meaningful and comprehensive responses.

Closed-ended questions

Closed-ended questions typically elicit brief, specific answers and are often used to gather factual information or confirm details. These questions are framed in a way that limits the response to a yes/no, a single word, or a specific option. They are essential for obtaining precise, to-the-point information.

Here are some examples of closed-ended questions:

"Did you attend the meeting yesterday?"

"Is the project due by the end of this week?"

"Do you prefer the red or blue design?"

"Have you ever visited Paris before?"

Closed-ended questions are useful when seeking specific facts, confirming details, or steering the conversation in a particular direction. However, they may limit the opportunity for the speaker to provide extensive insights or express their thoughts and emotions.

Use open-ended questions well, and you can allow them to delve deeper into a topic, widen their thoughts, and reflect on their own thoughts and feelings. In a cross-cultural situation, however, it's equally important to use closed-ended questions to clarify what has been said to ensure that you and your team have a comprehensive understanding of the speaker's perspective.

Active listening is a multifaceted process that involves showing attentive presence, demonstrating understanding, and engaging the speaker with thoughtful questions. By incorporating these three steps into your communication, you can foster deeper connections, build trust, and enhance the quality of your interactions with others.

Be mindful, however, to avoid jumping to conclusions or making judgments based on your own assumptions. Instead, use questions to explore the speaker's perspective without bias.

We'll dig deeper into active listening in Chapter 5.

4. Conflict resolution

Conflict is inevitable in any team, and in a multicultural setting, diverse perspectives can escalate conflicts if not managed effectively. As we learned in the team development stages section earlier, it's important for a facilitator to skillfully navigate the team through the storming stage. A facilitator skilled in conflict resolution can mediate conflicts, encourage understanding, and promote harmonious relationships within the team.

Adaptability is key. A skilled facilitator must possess the ability to modify strategies, plans, and behaviors to suit changing circumstances and diverse cultural context by swiftly adjusting their approach based on the needs of the team.

In a diverse team, cultural differences can sometimes be at the root of conflicts. A facilitator with conflict resolution skills understands these triggers and proactively addresses potential areas of disagreement before they escalate.

For example, a disagreement might arise regarding a project deadline. The facilitator identifies that differing attitudes toward time management are the source of the conflict and addresses it by facilitating a dialogue that leads to a compromise acceptable to all parties.

A skilled facilitator also encourages open and constructive dialogue to resolve conflicts. They ensure that team members express their concerns, thoughts, and feelings in a respectful and understanding manner, aiming for a mutually beneficial resolution.

Additionally, a facilitator can use discussion tools to bring everyone on the same page, visualize how the discussion is going, and problem-solve or bring conflict to consensus.

Remember, a skilled facilitator stays neutral, and manages the process of discussions to maximize the synergy of the diverse team. Discussion tools are helpful aids to do that.

Seven discussion tools

Let me introduce seven discussion tools that strategy consultants often use, that are useful for effective facilitation in a global team.

Logic tree: a brainstorming tool

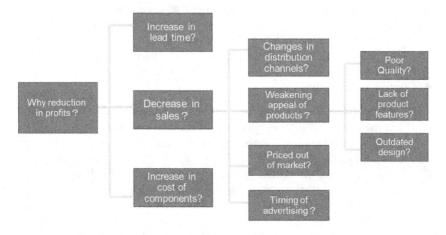

Explanation of logic tree

What it is

A logic tree is often used in brainstorming, and it is a visual tool that helps organize and structure complex information, identify potential solutions or outcomes, and guide the reasoning process. It's a hierarchical diagram resembling a tree, whereby each branch represents a possible option, decision, or condition, leading to further branches or nodes that break down the potential consequences or actions associated with each option. This method allows for systematic exploration and evaluation of different paths or scenarios related to a particular problem or objective.

Purpose

- Structuring information: A logic tree organizes information in a logical and systematic manner, making it easier to see the big picture, analyze, and navigate through a complex issue.
- Identifying options: It helps in generating and visualizing various potential options or courses of action related to a problem or goal.
- Developing hypotheses: By mapping out potential consequences or outcomes for each option, it aids in determining the potential impact and risks associated with each choice. The visual representation of different paths and outcomes leads to hypothesis development by providing a clear overview of the available options and their implications.

Process

1. Set the problem or "issue"

   Clearly define the problem you're addressing. In strategy consultants' terms, we call it "issue." So logic tree is sometimes called "issue tree." Understanding the scope of the issue helps in focusing the logic tree.

2. Determine main branches (first layer)

   Identify the main options or decisions related to the issue. These will form the main branches of the logic tree. Typically, these options are Mutually Exclusive and Collectively Exhaustive (or MECE). (You may recall from Chapter 2 that these concepts are often used in logical thinking. Mutually Exclusive means that events can't happen simultaneously, while Collectively Exhaustive means all possible outcomes are considered.) Ask "Why did this happen?" or "How can we improve?" and brainstorm for some causes of the issues in a manner as MECE as possible.

3. Break down each option (second layer)

   For each main branch, break down the option into sub-branches, representing potential actions, conditions, or outcomes associated with that option.

4. Continue to subdivide (third layer and on)

   Subdivide the sub-branches further, detailing the consequences, conditions, or steps related to each action until the analysis is sufficiently comprehensive. Keep asking "Why?" or "How?" to drill down to find the true cause or specific actions to take.

5. Assign probabilities or weights

   If applicable, assign probabilities or weights to different branches or nodes to account for uncertainty or likelihood of occurrence for various outcomes. When you come up with specific ideas, choose the factor that has the greatest impact and most realistic to implement.

6. Analyze

   Assess each path in the logic tree, considering the potential outcomes and associated probabilities. Analyze the overall implications of each option and potential hypothesis. When you come up with specific ideas, choose the factor which has the greatest impact and most realistic to implement.

7. Develop hypothesis

Use the insights gained from the logic tree analysis to develop the hypothesis, considering the potential impact, risks, and probabilities associated with each option.

Affinity diagram: an information sorting tool

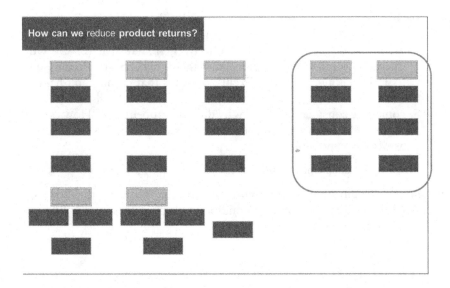

Explanation of affinity diagram

What it is

An affinity diagram is a technique used in project management, business analysis, and problem-solving to organize and categorize large amounts of unstructured data or ideas into meaningful groups based on their natural relationships or similarities. Hence the name, "affinity." It's a visual tool that helps teams organize complex information into categories, so that the information is more manageable and provides insights for further decision-making.

Purpose

• Organizing information: It helps in organizing a vast amount of information, ideas, or data into manageable groups.

- Identifying patterns and themes: Patterns, themes, and trends become more evident by grouping related items, allowing for deeper analysis.
- Generating insights: By visually clustering related items, insights and potential solutions emerge, aiding in problem-solving and decision-making.

Process

1. Collect data/ideas

   This is a brainstorming stage. Gather all relevant data, ideas, or information related to the topic of interest.

   With the facilitator's lead, each participant thinks of solutions and writes them on a sticky note. Make sure you write just *one* idea on each sticky note, because you will organize those sticky notes in the next process. Additionally, do not write your name on the sticky notes, because when you are brainstorming, you want to eliminate any potential cause for judgment.

2. Grouping similar ideas

   The facilitator encourages participants to put all the finished sticky notes on a wall or a white board, or a large flipchart.

   Begin by reviewing and sorting the collected data through active group discussion. Look for commonalities, similarities, or related themes among the items. Group these based on these similarities by moving sticky notes around.

   There is still no evaluation or critiquing of ideas at this point yet.

3. Create affinity groups

   Establish distinct groups or categories for the related items. These groups should represent overarching themes or concepts that encompass the items within them.

4. Label the groups

   Assign labels or headers to each group that clearly describe the common theme or concept that unifies the items in that group.

5. Refine and revise

   Continuously review and refine the groups to ensure that the items within each group truly belong together based on meaningful relationships. Adjustments can be made as needed. When a group discussion is facilitated effectively, one team member's idea could trigger another idea.

6. Create the affinity diagram

Physically organize the grouped sticky notes and finalize the groups and their labels. If it's a virtual meeting, this can also be done by using specialized software for digital visualization.

7. Review and interpret

Once the diagram is complete, review it as a team and interpret the insights derived from the grouped items. Discuss potential actions, decisions, or next steps based on the insights gained from the affinity diagram.

Payoff matrix: an evaluation tool

Steps	Example
1. Define the scope of the process and set the start and end points	⌜○○○Process⌟ • From receive ○○ order to delivery of ○○ Start — End
2. Capture the major flow and remember to map the actual, "as is" process	Major steps Actual steps and decision points
3. Use symbols to represent activities, decision points, and direction of the flow	Start — End
4. Clarify which department or work area is responsible for various sections of the process	Dept A Start Dept B Dept C

Explanation of payoff matrix

What it is

A payoff matrix is a strategic tool used in game theory, economics, and decision analysis to represent the possible outcomes of a decision or strategic choices. It allows you to take multiple alternatives and narrow them down. It is a natural next step after brainstorming ideas using the affinity diagram.

The payoff matrix can help leaders assess and choose the most suitable course of action from a set of alternatives. Decision-makers can weigh the payoffs associated with different actions and prioritize options based on their goals, risks, and desired outcomes. By clearly presenting the payoffs associated with each possible combination of actions, decision-makers can discern which strategies yield the most favorable outcomes. This information is pivotal in making informed decisions and prioritizing actions that align with organizational objectives or personal goals.

Purpose

- Strategic decision-making

  It provides a structured framework for decision-makers to analyze their options and potential outcomes in strategic interactions.

- Identifying optimal strategies

  By analyzing the matrix, participants can identify optimal strategies that maximize their payoffs or outcomes given the actions of others.

- Understanding interactions

  It helps in understanding how the choices and actions of each participant affect not only their own outcomes but also the outcomes of others in a competitive or cooperative setting.

Process

First, list ideas/solutions using brainstorming or affinity diagram. Do not evaluate ideas at this point.

1. Assign payoff values

   Determine two key criteria to evaluate the options, such as impact vs. feasibility, time vs. cost, or profitability vs. time to implement. This is the most important step, as it determines how you are going to evaluate options. Get this wrong, and your chosen action plans will not be effective.

2. Construct the matrix

   Draw two axes and assign the criteria. You should have four quadrants. Make sure that the upper right quadrant is the most optimal option. Why? Because usually, people's perception is that situations improve or progress from bottom left toward upper right.

3. Plot ideas

Facilitate discussion to locate the ideas into the four quadrants. Sticky notes come in handy here.

4. Analyze and interpret

Analyze the matrix to determine the optimal strategies.
Make the most optimal ideas/solutions in the top right corner the highest priority items (for further research, data collection or implementation).

Process map: a process improvement tool

Steps	Example
Determine the scope of the process and set the start and end points	⌜OOOProcess⌟ • From receive OO order to delivery of OO Start — End
First capture the major flow and remember to map the actual, "as is" process	Major steps Actual steps and decision points
Use symbols to represent activities, decision points, and direction of the flow	Start — End
Clarify which department or work area is responsible for various sections of the process	Dept A Start — End Dept B Dept C

Explanation of process map

What it is

A process map, also known as a process flow chart, is a visual representation that outlines the steps, activities, interactions, and decisions involved in a certain business activity. It helps in understanding and analyzing a process to identify areas for improvement, streamline operations, and enhance overall efficiency. Process mapping is widely used in various fields such as business, engineering, healthcare, and project management.

Purpose

- Visualize the whole process

  A process map provides a clear, visual representation of a process, enabling stakeholders to understand the flow and sequence of activities involved.

- Identify improvement areas in the process

  It facilitates the analysis of a process to identify bottlenecks, redundancies, or inefficiencies. This understanding serves as a foundation for process improvement initiatives.

- Standardization and consistency

  Process maps help in standardizing procedures and ensuring that tasks are performed consistently, leading to a higher level of quality and reliability.

- Communication and training

  They serve as valuable tools for communicating processes to employees, clients, or stakeholders. Process maps are also used for training new employees and ensuring everyone understands their roles and responsibilities.

- Compliance and documentation

  In regulated industries, process maps are essential for compliance with standards and regulations. They also aid in documenting processes for audit purposes.

Process

1. Define the scope of the process

   Clearly define the specific process you want to map. Understand its purpose, objectives, and the desired outcomes. Set the start and end points.

2. Capture the major flow

   Collect all relevant data and information about the process. This may include interviews, observations, existing documentation, and data analysis.

Remember to map the "as-is" process, not the "should be" process. The biggest pitfall many fall into is that they start mixing in "should be" process, as they discuss further. Then, you can't detect true bottlenecks, redundancy, or inefficiency. The facilitator needs to pay close attention to avoid this mistake.

3. Identify steps and activities

Break down the process into distinct steps, or activities. Use shapes or symbols to represent each step, making the flowchart easier to understand.
Connect the steps by using arrows to indicate the direction of the process. Make sure to connect each step in the order it occurs. Ensure the flow is logical and reflects the actual progression of the process.
Add decision points where the process could take different paths based on specific conditions. Branch the flow accordingly.

4. Review, validate, and finalize

Review the process map with team members to validate its accuracy and completeness. Incorporate feedback and make necessary revisions.
Finalize the process map, ensuring it is clear, easy to understand, and accurately represents the process, and clarify which department or work area is responsible for various sections of the process for further discussion or improvement.

SWOT analysis: a strategy development tool

Strengths	Weaknesses
Opportunities	Threats

Explanation of SWOT analysis

What it is

SWOT analysis is a strategy development tool often used by strategy consultants to identify and evaluate organizations' internal strengths and weaknesses, as well as external opportunities and threats. The acronym "SWOT" stands for Strengths, Weaknesses, Opportunities, and Threats. I personally use this framework quite often when I conduct strategy consulting for my clients. It is also a great discussion tool for any facilitator to facilitate high-level discussions. By conducting a SWOT analysis, organizations can make more informed decisions, develop effective strategies, and improve their overall performance and competitiveness in the market.

Following is a breakdown of each component and the process of conducting a SWOT analysis.

Strengths (S)

Strengths are internal attributes and resources that give an organization a competitive advantage. These could include skilled personnel, strong brand reputation, advanced technology, efficient processes, or a loyal customer base.

Weaknesses (W)

Weaknesses are internal factors that hinder an organization's ability to compete effectively. These could include inadequate resources, lack of expertise, poor infrastructure, or inefficient processes.

Opportunities (O)

Opportunities are external factors that an organization can capitalize on to enhance its performance or competitive position. These could be emerging markets, advancements in technology, changes in regulations, or partnerships.

Threats (T)

Threats are external factors that can negatively affect an organization's performance or viability. These could include economic downturns, intense competition, changes in consumer behavior, or legal and regulatory challenges.

Purpose

The purpose of conducting a SWOT analysis lies in its ability to provide valuable insights and strategic clarity for organizations. Following are the key purposes of a SWOT analysis.

- Strategic planning and decision-making

  SWOT analysis helps organizations understand their internal strengths and weaknesses, as well as the external opportunities and threats they face. This understanding forms the foundation for developing effective strategic plans and making informed decisions.

- Identify competitive advantages

  By evaluating internal strengths, an organization can identify what sets it apart from competitors. These strengths can be leveraged to gain a competitive edge in the market and capitalize on opportunities.

- Risk assessment and mitigation

  The analysis of weaknesses and threats enables organizations to identify potential risks and vulnerabilities. With this knowledge, they can develop strategies to mitigate these risks and develop contingency plans to safeguard the organization's interests.

- Resource allocation and optimization

  Understanding the internal strengths and weaknesses allows organizations to allocate resources more efficiently. They can invest in areas that play to their strengths and work on improving or addressing weaknesses to optimize resource utilization.

- Goal alignment and focus

  SWOT analysis helps in aligning an organization's goals and objectives with its capabilities and the external environment. It guides the organization toward setting achievable goals that align with its strengths and opportunities.

- Problem-solving and innovation

  The analysis facilitates problem-solving by helping organizations identify the root causes of issues, especially those related to weaknesses and threats. It also stimulates innovative thinking by encouraging the exploration of new ways to capitalize on strengths and opportunities.

- Facilitate communication and collaboration

  SWOT analysis often involves multiple stakeholders within an organization. It encourages collaboration and communication among different teams or departments, ensuring a more holistic view of the organization's position in the market.

- Change management and adaptability

    In a rapidly changing business environment, understanding weaknesses and threats becomes crucial for change management. A SWOT analysis can help organizations adapt to changing circumstances and make timely adjustments to their strategies and operations.

- Performance evaluation and benchmarking

    After implementing strategies derived from the SWOT analysis, organizations can use it as a benchmark to evaluate performance and measure progress. Comparing actual outcomes with the initially identified strengths, weaknesses, opportunities, and threats helps with continuous improvement.

Process

1. Define the objective

    Clearly define the objective or area of focus for the SWOT analysis. This could be a specific project, a new market entry, a product launch, or an overall assessment of the organization.

2. Gather information

    Collect relevant data and information about the internal and external aspects of the organization. This can include reviewing financial statements, market research, customer feedback, employee feedback, and industry reports.

3. Identify strengths and weaknesses (internal analysis)

    Assess the internal aspects of the organization to identify its strengths and weaknesses. This might involve evaluating the organization's resources, capabilities, processes, and overall performance.

4. Identify opportunities and threats (external analysis)

    Evaluate the external environment to identify opportunities and threats. Analyze market trends, competitive landscapes, economic conditions, regulatory changes, and other factors that could affect the organization.

5. Cross-functional collaboration

    Involve a diverse group of stakeholders – including managers, employees, and subject matter experts – to gain different perspectives and insights during the analysis.

6. Create a SWOT matrix

Create a SWOT matrix to visualize and organize the identified strengths, weaknesses, opportunities, and threats. This matrix allows for a clear comparison and identification of strategic options.

7. Strategy development

Based on the SWOT analysis, develop strategies that leverage strengths and opportunities while mitigating weaknesses and threats. These strategies should align with the organization's goals and objectives.

8. Action plan

Develop a detailed action plan with specific steps, responsibilities, time-lines, and metrics to implement the chosen strategies effectively.

Force field diagram: a change catalyst tool

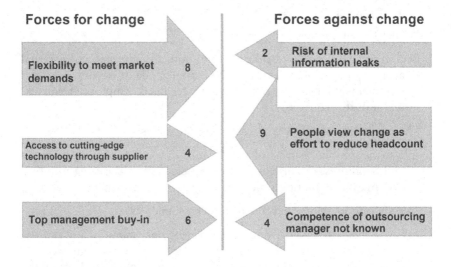

Explanation of Force Field Diagram

What it is

A Force Field Analysis (FFA) is a strategic management tool used to analyze and visualize the driving forces (factors that promote change) and restraining forces (factors that hinder change) that influence a proposed change or decision within an organization. Developed by

Kurt Lewin, this technique helps in understanding the factors that can support or hinder the successful implementation of a change initiative.[2]

It illustrates the different forces affecting a particular decision or change. It uses arrows to depict the magnitude and direction of each force, indicating whether it's driving the change forward or resisting it.[3]

The Force Field Diagram helps visualize the balance between driving and restraining forces, assisting in decision-making and change management by providing a structured approach to analyzing the dynamics of change within an organization.[4]

Purpose

The main purposes of using FFA are:

- Identifying factors: It helps identify and list all the factors (forces) for and against a proposed change or decision.
- Assessing impact: It allows for the assessment of the relative strength and impact of each force influencing the change initiative.
- Decision-making: It helps in making informed decisions by evaluating whether the driving forces outweigh the restraining forces, or vice versa.
- Planning interventions: It aids in planning interventions to bolster the driving forces and mitigate the restraining forces to facilitate successful change implementation.

Process

1. Identify the change or decision

    Clearly define the change or decision you want to analyze. It could be anything from implementing a new process to introducing a new product to altering organizational policies.

2. Identify driving and restraining forces

    Brainstorm and list all the factors or forces that are driving the change forward (positive forces).

    Similarly, identify the factors or forces that are resisting the change (negative forces).

3. Indicate weight

    Assess and assign a numerical value or weight (e.g., on a scale of 1–10) to each force to indicate its relative strength or impact. Higher numbers indicate the strength of the force in favor of or against the desired change.

4. Draw the Force Field Diagram

Draw a "T" and list the positive forces on the left and negative forces on the right.

Draw arrows pointing in opposite directions, with the width of the arrows representing the relative strength of each force.

5. Analyze and interpret

Assess the diagram to determine whether the driving forces outweigh the restraining forces, or vice versa.

Based on the analysis, decide whether to proceed with the change, modify the plan, or take appropriate actions to strengthen driving forces or mitigate restraining forces.

PPM analysis: a portfolio project management analysis tool

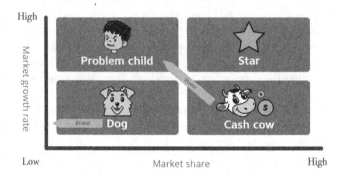

Explanation of PPM analysis

What it is

Portfolio project management analysis, or PPM analysis, is commonly used to evaluate and prioritize a portfolio of projects within an organization. It's also called "BCG Matrix," as one of world's top consulting firms, Boston Consulting Group developed this model.

By following the PPM analysis process, organizations can make informed decisions about which projects to undertake, how to allocate resources, and how to manage risks and returns effectively, resulting in a well-structured and value-driven project portfolio.

PPM analysis consists of four elements:

1. Cash cow

A cash cow (sometimes called "money tree") represents a project or product with a high market share in a low-growth market.

These are established projects or products that generate consistent cash flows and profits, typically requiring minimal investment.

Cash cows provide the financial stability needed to support and invest in other projects or products in the portfolio.

2. Star

A star is a project or product with a high market share in a high-growth market.

Stars are projects or products in a growth phase that have a significant market share and potential for high returns.

Investment in stars is crucial to maintain and increase market share and profitability as the market grows.

3. Problem child (question mark)

A problem child (sometimes called a "question mark") is a project or product with low market share in a high-growth market.

Problem children are projects or products with potential but currently low market share. They often require significant investment to become stars.

Decide whether to invest more to turn them into stars or discontinue them if the potential doesn't justify the investment.

4. Dog

A dog (sometimes called "underdog") is a project or product with low market share in a low-growth market.

Dogs are low-performing projects or products with minimal market share and limited growth potential.

Consider discontinuing or divesting from these projects to allocate resources more effectively to other high-potential projects.

Purpose

The overall purpose of PPM Analysis is to ensure that projects align with organizational goals, that resources are utilized efficiently, and that the overall portfolio delivers the maximum value and return on investment (ROI).

- Alignment with organizational strategy: Ensure that the projects in the portfolio align with the organization's strategic objectives and goals.
- Resource optimization: Efficiently allocate resources by selecting projects that maximize resource utilization and minimize conflicts.
- Risk management: Identify and manage risks associated with the projects to mitigate potential negative impacts on the organization.

- ROI: Evaluate the potential return on investment for each project and the overall portfolio to ensure the optimal use of organizational resources.
- Balanced portfolio: Maintain a balanced portfolio that includes projects of varying risk levels, timelines, and potential benefits to diversify organizational investments and outcomes.

Process

1. Identify all projects

   Identify and categorize all projects within the portfolio based on their market share and market growth rate.

2. Place projects

   Place each project in the appropriate quadrant of the matrix (cash cow, star, problem child, or dog) based on its market share and market growth.

3. Analysis and decision-making

   Analyze the positioning of each project and determine appropriate strategies for each category, considering investment, divestment, or other strategic actions. Develop strategies for each category:

   Cash cows: Focus on maximizing cash flow and efficiency.
   Stars: Invest to maintain or increase market share and profitability.
   Problem children: Decide on investment or divestment based on potential and alignment with organizational goals.
   Dogs: Consider divestment or consolidation of resources into higher potential projects.

* * *

Facilitating discussions among global teams is a complex task due to diverse perspectives, cultural differences, and potential communication challenges. The seven frameworks I introduced provide a structured approach and visual guidelines that serve as effective discussion tools to navigate these complexities and ensure effective communication and collaboration, especially during the storming stage of the team.

The structure helps a facilitator maintain focus and prevent discussions from veering off-track. It also improves clarity in discussions because of their visual nature, and keeps everyone on the same page.

Moreover, well-structured frameworks enhance engagement by providing a clear agenda and purpose for the discussion. Team members are more likely to actively participate and contribute when they understand the context and goals of the discussion. This engagement is essential for meaningful interactions and decision-making, and frameworks help facilitators improve diverse team's engagement.

In a global team, conflicts may arise due to cultural differences or diverse opinions. A structured approach to resolving conflicts and making decisions helps maintain team harmony and progress toward project goals.

Make sure that all team members, regardless of their location or position, have an opportunity to contribute. This promotes an inclusive environment and ensures that diverse perspectives are considered, enhancing decision quality.

Using frameworks may take some practice. But it allows facilitators to develop and enhance their facilitation skills. It provides a guide for effectively managing discussions, improving communication techniques, and handling diverse groups. Over time, facilitators become more adept at managing global discussions.

However, even with effective frameworks, there is one last piece of the puzzle that's crucial in a global team.

Let's get back to Day 3 of the workshop for H Corp, when participants experienced the storming stage right in the middle of a group discussion.

* * *

Day 3 starts with a review of Day 1 and Day 2.

All participants are equipped with key facilitation skills, warmed up to each other, and ready to get their hands dirty on their actual business challenges. They have four hours to discuss and come up with their action plans. In the afternoon, they will present their action plans to H Corp's top management, when President Ozaki will provide immediate go/no-go decisions.

It seems the forming stage has passed after Day 1 and Day 2, and everyone has become comfortable expressing their opinions and digging into deeper discussions.

Then, it happens.

"With such shallow discussions, our business won't change at all!" Francois in Group 5 exclaims, right before they break for lunchtime. "It's the people who drive the change!"

"Thank you!" Vladmir said, agreeing with Francois for the first time.

Almost all the participants in the room turn to Group 5 with surprised looks on their faces.

Most surprised is Robert, an American sales manager, in Group 5.

Robert doesn't hesitate to show his frustration. "I don't understand what is so shallow about it! There are good examples and valuable insights coming out of the discussions!"

He continues, "In the brainstorming about past success factors, we came up with things like 'product differentiation in terms of functionality,' 'high convenience,' and 'establishing relationships with key customers.' These were written on large sticky notes as keywords, and success factors were extracted from them. Nobody criticized these points."

Missing piece

What do you think happened here?

There could be various reasons, but the biggest issue was that this group did not allocate time for sharing context.

Context refers to what's behind that information, such as who struggled how; how they got buy-in from the management internally (since you need to persuade not only outsiders, such as customers, but also insiders, such as top management and your own teammates who have different interests, and/or other departments that have a conflict of interest); and how they solved problems with customers. Without this context, discussions moved functionally, grouping everything under headings like "functionality" and "relationships." That's why some people might have felt as though it was "superficial."

In a nutshell, the information was shared, but the context wasn't.

Communication involves not just information but also elements of context.

As we learned in the previous chapters, Japan is one of the few High Context societies in the world. Information sharing is essential for people to understand each other, but the importance of information is relatively low, compared to the context.

On the other hand, countries like Germany, Switzerland, the Scandinavian countries, and the United States belong to Low Context culture zones, where information takes precedence over context.

In brainstorming and processes like affinity diagrams, information comes up, but if there is hardly any time allocated for sharing context, it ends up being quite Low Context. As a result, people from Low Context cultures might have understood it, but for High Context participants, it might have seemed superficial.

At H Corp, Robert, being from the United States, was Low Context, and more information-driven. Vladmir from Russia and Francois from France were both High Context, so there were differences in how they perceived the discussion.

But it goes way beyond country differences.

Back to the workshop.

* * *

Robert looks quite frustrated. Some participants seem to agree with his points, and others have no clue.

I decide to go back to the earlier agenda, and emphasize the importance of cross-cultural models, and ask for their thoughts.

Carol speaks up. "So, while High Context sounds cool, you don't care much about reasoning, but you just spend time with them? What do you think?"

Carol turns to Pablo.

Pablo responds by turning to HR manager Wang. "How about helping us, High Context–oriented Wang?" Pablo says this with a chuckle to lighten up his tone.

Wang has been sitting relatively quiet, but now that he is directly called upon, he shares his valuable insights, as if he has been given permission to openly express his opinion.

I'm in the HR department, and people in such roles tend to become context-oriented. They also tend to argue a lot. Those on the front lines are also somewhat High Context. They live within each piece of data. But it sometimes creates friction. Proposals from strategy consultants like McKinsey are very Low Context, but even if they have excellent suggestions, they might not be accepted by the front lines if context is missing. So, in the real business world where time is a constraint, bridging this gap becomes a significant issue. Unfortunately, in global business, we're heading toward Low Context, which is something that High Context people struggle with. Even in technology development, internationalization is unavoidable. So we can't define cultural differences by drawing lines between countries. But it exists everywhere. We all need to walk toward each other.

Wang stops there, and looks at me. "Am I understanding correctly, Natsuyo san?"

"Well said."

I look around the room, and they are all nodding in agreement.

* * *

Communication in culturally diverse teams is an art

High Context communication is often treated as an art. Such communication binds people, creates cohesion, has a long lifespan, and doesn't change much. Low Context communication doesn't have the bonding effect and is more susceptible to change.

Is there a strategy to balance these two clearly contrasting demands, a desire for change (Low Context orientation) and a desire for stability (High Context orientation)?

The 3-Step Process, the 3As, is the answer.

Diversity and inclusion are key attributes to any high-performing team.

As the world becomes increasingly interconnected, global teams are becoming more prevalent in organizations. Leading a diverse global team can be a challenging task, particularly when team members are spread across different time zones, cultures, and languages. When a culturally diverse group of people comes together, they often fail to really connect with people "who aren't like me" and work collaboratively toward a common goal.

Part of this is down to a lack of cross-cultural empathy, or our ability to put ourselves in the shoes of others and to understand what another person is experiencing. It's an understandable challenge. When someone has had a completely different upbringing or set of experiences than our own, or there exists a language and cultural barrier, how can we adequately respond to their views – and how can we even listen effectively?

Cultural diversity isn't just a matter of ethnicity, gender, and sexual orientation; it's also about a group of individuals who have worked in different sectors or lived or worked in multiple countries – bringing with them different experiences and viewpoints.

All these diverse experiences can actually work powerfully together when harnessed in the right way by the right leader. But if handled poorly, there could be chaos.

With the 3As in mind, equip yourself with global facilitation skills. Stay neutral, manage the process of the team, bring out each team member's strength and create synergy, bridge cultural differences, and maximize the team productivity.

It takes practice and patience. But when you implement what you learned in this chapter, you'll find the fourth A: Amazing.

Notes

1 Bruce W. Tuckman, "Developmental sequence in small groups," *Psychological Bulletin* 63, no. 6 (June 1965): 384–99, https://doi.org/10.1037/h0022100.
2 Kurt Lewin, "Frontiers in group dynamics: Concept, method and reality in social science; social equilibria and social change," *Human Relations* 1, no. 1 (June 1947): 5–41, https://doi.org/10.1177/001872674700100103.
3 Kurt Lewin, "Frontiers in group dynamics: Concept, method and reality in social science; social equilibria and social change," *Human Relations* 1, no. 1 (June 1947): 5–41, https://doi.org/10.1177/001872674700100103.
4 Kurt Lewin, "Frontiers in group dynamics: Concept, method and reality in social science; social equilibria and social change," *Human Relations* 1, no. 1 (June 1947): 5–41, https://doi.org/10.1177/001872674700100103.

Chapter 5

Message heard and acted upon in one-on-one communication

My husband Rob loves British comedies.

While he's watching them and innocently laughing at British humor, I'm often observing and analyzing cultural differences. Occupational disease, I know.

In Japan, where I'm from, comedies often have a more animated and exaggerated tone, emphasizing physical comedy and expressive gestures.

I enjoy American comedies, as well. They often feature larger-than-life characters, sometimes exaggerated or stereotypical. They typically have a faster pace, and the humor is more overt, with punchlines and gags.

British humor, on the other hand, is known for its deadpan humor and slower pacing. It often emphasizes wit, satire, irony, and absurdity. Sometimes, I find British humor funny; other times, I don't get it.

But what I'm overly impressed at is their sophisticated and clever dialogues.

There is one particular scene in the British comedy from the 80s called *Yes, Minister* that shows how a question can completely redirect the conversation. See below for the witty dialogue between the characters Bernard and Prime Minister Hacker.

[Bernard pulls Prime Minister Hacker away for a private conversation.]

Hacker: You just said that the Foreign Office was keeping something from me! How do you know if you don't know?

Bernard: I don't know specifically what, Prime Minister, but I do know that the Foreign Office always keeps everything from everybody. It's normal practice.

Hacker: Who does know?

Bernard: May I just clarify the question? You are asking who would know what it is that I don't know and you don't know but the Foreign Office knows that they know that they are keeping from you so that you don't know but they do know and all we know

DOI: 10.4324/9781003455615-6

	there is something we don't know and we want to know but we don't know what because we don't know! Is that it?
Hacker:	May I clarify the question? Who knows Foreign Office secrets, apart from the Foreign Office?
Bernard:	Oh, that's easy: only the Kremlin.[1]

The quality of questions drastically changes the course of action.

As a strategic global presentation coach, I've been training hundreds of global leaders through corporate training and workshops, but I love working with private clients. I truly enjoy uncovering their stories, learning how they got where they are, and most importantly, Why.

When you are in a private coaching session with me, you'll notice that I ask a lot of questions, especially in the first few sessions. My job as a presentation coach is not to tell my client what to say, but to bring out a hidden gem, ignite the spark, and invite them to discover their own story. I uncover, and you discover. Only then does your story sparkle as a one-of-a-kind story.

And the only way to achieve it is by asking GOOD questions.

GOOD questions have the power to spark curiosity and prompt to dig deeper, search for answers within, encourage critical thinking, foster creativity, drive progress, enhance communication, deepen understanding . . . I can keep going . . . and ultimately contribute to personal and professional growth. Learning to craft GOOD questions is a skill that can positively affect various aspects of our lives and the lives of those around us.

As a global leader, you must have many opportunities to engage in one-on-one conversations, as often as in a group or team setting. In these conversations, you may clarify job roles, responsibilities, and expectations through one-on-one conversations. You may have periodical performance reviews and feedback sessions. You may meet with team members individually to discuss their career development. Sometimes you may need to address conflicts or disputes privately. You may act as a coach or mentor and offer guidance, or you may have some casual check-ins.

How are you building trust on a personal level?

Are you asking GOOD questions enough?

Why should you care about GOOD questions?

What are GOOD questions, anyway?

Let's take a deep dive.

Why quality questions matter

Communication is not just about speaking but also about listening. It's a two-way street.

Especially when you are working with High Context people, they have a lot more information in the part of the iceberg you don't see.

So it becomes an important skill to learn to *listen to what is meant instead of what is said*, and also to read the atmosphere and uncover what hasn't yet been said.

The key to do that is in asking GOOD questions.

The quality of GOOD questions could lead to big differences in people's performances, businesses, and lives.

* * *

I have worked with a life coach in the past. Yes, I was the coachee. Sometimes you need to sit on the other side of the table, right?

In one of our sessions, my coach and I were discussing my life situation. I have a preteen daughter who goes to a private school and does competitive figure skating. I used to actively compete in ballroom Latin dancing, but I was taking a pause for more than a year, because most of my money and time go to my daughter. My priority is different now. I need to work harder and smarter to support her, and spend as much time with her as possible because she will leave home for college in several years.

I explained all this to my coach, who asked, "Are you happy with the situation now?"

I couldn't answer immediately.

"Well . . . ," I said, "I guess . . . yes, I'm dedicating myself to raise my precious daughter while working full force. But . . . happy . . . ahm. Happy. Hmmm."

By asking this GOOD question, my coach forced me to take a closer look. The way I had to wrestle with my response was revealing.

"If you had all the freedom and no limitation whatsoever," she prompted, "what makes you happy then?"

"Dancing." I answered immediately this time, and that surprised me.

I knew dancing gave me joy, but I didn't quite realize how much I *needed* to get dancing back in my life. The second question dug deeper below my iceberg, and surfaced what I really wanted and needed.

My coach continued.

"Great! When do you want to go back to dancing?"

I went back into the un-committal zone again.

"Well, . . . I need time and money to resume dancing. Right now, both go to my daughter."

"So, you need time and money to resume dancing, and that's why you haven't been dancing for more than a year. But dancing gives you true joy. Correct? What can you do to save time and money?"

Before having this conversation with my coach, I'd written off dancing entirely. With this framing, I started to think in ways I hadn't allowed myself before. But I was still hesitant, seeing things as all or nothing. "If my daughter cuts back on skating, maybe I could . . . ."

"How often do you want to dance?" My coach interjected. "Once a week? Three times a week?

"Even one lesson a week would make me happy," I said.

"Just once a week. That's not a lot of time or money, is it?"

"You're right."

"So what can you do to save time and money, just enough for one lesson a week?"

Put to me this way, I shifted away from "this isn't possible for me without giving up something I'm unwilling to give up." I started seeing options. "If we cut down on eating at a restaurant from twice a week to once a week, that might do!"

"Great! When are you going to book your first dance lesson?"

"Oh, ahm . . . . I'll reach out today . . . ? And book a lesson for . . . next week?"

"Fantastic. So you are going to cut down on dining out, reach out to your dance teacher today, and book a lesson for next week. Yes?"

"Yes!"

The following week, I was back in the dance studio for the first time in over a year. When I stepped into the studio and saw my teacher sitting there waiting for me, I cried. Tears of joy, of course. I am so glad I went back, and it truly felt like my life was turning back up again.

* * *

This coach's questions got me tapping deeper into myself, seeking wider options, and moving forward with commitment.

Deeper, Wider, Forward.

These are the three directions that high-quality GOOD questions can take you in.

The quality of a question can influence how individuals perceive a situation, solve problems, and collaborate with others.

For global leaders, understanding and harnessing the power of asking high-quality GOOD questions is of paramount importance because it affects their leadership effectiveness – and ultimately, their organizational success.

Now, what are high-quality GOOD questions?

That's a good question to start!

Four types of questions

First, when I say GOOD questions, there are also questions that are not good.

Questions are categorized into four types: light questions, bad questions, heavy questions, and GOOD questions.

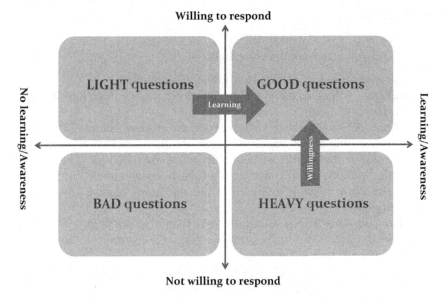

Explanation of four types of questions

The vertical axis of Figure shows how willing the person answering the question is to answer.

For that person, the position on the vertical axis is determined by whether answering that question is fun, thought-provoking, or makes them feel good.

The horizontal axis shows how deep the insights you can receive from their answer to the question. The further to the right, the more insightful and has a high potential for growth. Conversely, moving to the left means fewer insights.

Almost all questions should fall into one of the four quadrants.

How about "stupid questions?", you may ask. They say there are no stupid questions, right? Well, if there are, they should fall under "bad" questions.

Now, let's take a closer look at the four questions.

Light questions

Light questions break the ice.

Simply put, they are questions that improve the relationship between the asker and the answerer.

Questions like,

"How was your weekend?"
"Did you watch football last night?"

Light questions are "getting-to-know-you" questions.

People are willing to answer light questions, and you can have a great conversation.

Imagine questions that a well-experienced veteran salesperson would ask when meeting a new customer. These are questions that allow you to find out about the person without disturbing their feelings. The person answering will also literally answer in a light-hearted manner.

But the answers to light questions are not going to give you crucial information or deep insights.

What you need to pay attention to is that it is the person who was asked the question – not the person who asked the question – who decides whether it is a light question or not.

Even if you asked a question with the intention of improving the relationship with the other person and ended up worsening the relationship as a result, it is not a light question but a bad question.

Asking about something that makes the person happy during the conversation also tends to be a light question. For example, many people are happy to talk about their successes in work, academics, or sports. In my case, if you ask me about cakes, I'd be happy to tell you all about them, from where to get the best cake to who is the hottest pastry chef in town.

Laying a foundation for GOOD questions

Many people unconsciously throw light questions in their conversations, but as a communication strategist, I incorporate light questions with intention.

Light questions are the building blocks for a good relationship with the other person.

When a good relationship isn't properly established, asking other questions can make the other person uncomfortable.

Personally, I have experienced this uncomfortable situation in the past.

One time I was casually browsing at a department store. At one store, I saw a floral dress I liked, and I was contemplating whether or not to buy it. Suddenly, from behind, a young female salesperson asked me with an innocent smile, "Where are you thinking about wearing this to?"

None of your business! I thought.

This salesperson and I don't know each other, and hadn't even exchanged a single word since I entered the store. Yet, I was suddenly questioned.

Why should I tell a personal thing to a total stranger?! It made me feel uncomfortable.

She might have just started the job and didn't know the proper customer service etiquette. She might have been taught by her manager that engaging with customers is important. And for her, asking that question might have been intended as a relatively light question. But just as I mentioned previously, the salesperson's intent only goes so far. As the person on the receiving end of the question, it was up to me whether or not the question was indeed "light."

A psychologist once said that questions are "one of the most powerful means to program your brain."

Questions have the power to compel thought. Even in a sudden question from someone with a relatively shallow relationship and you think "Why do I have to be asked that?", you find yourself pausing for a moment and thinking about that question. As a result, you may feel uncomfortable.

We should all be aware of the impact questions have on the other person. It's important to pay attention to whether the timing is right, if the relationship is established, if the question will make the other person feel unpleasant, etc.

Information gathering with light questions

To create appropriate questions, information gathering is essential.

In my presentation coaching sessions, I sometimes ask the person about important things they usually keep deep within themselves, such as their profound beliefs and values in life. However, if a good relationship hasn't been established yet, asking questions like, "Please tell me about the values you hold dear in your life," might surprise them or result in vague answers. That's why I utilize light questions before asking substantial ones. This is a necessary step to establish a good relationship with the client and better equips me to ask GOOD questions later.

For example, I ask about everything the person is willing to share about themselves first. Where they grew up, what they learned in school, the experiences they gained at work, the people, incidents, thoughts, and experiences that shaped their way of thinking, and so on. Of course, before coaching, I always make sure to check the client's company website or social media profiles and posts. This preliminary research allows me to gather information about the client's thinking patterns. Based on this research, I craft a series of light questions.

Also, as you repeatedly use light questions, you gradually acquire the words the person prefers to use. Every individual has a bias and tendency in the words they unconsciously use. And that choice of words reflects that person's values. While discussing past events, carefully listening to each word the person uses to describe why they perceive it as a success or failure, how they arrived at a certain conclusion, and how they express it provides material for creating GOOD questions later. The words that are repeated often become a crucial key to crafting GOOD questions.

Bad questions

Bad questions freeze the ice . . . .
   Questions like,

   "Aren't you getting married?"
   "How much money do you have in your bank account?"

These questions don't consider relationships. They often have negative and blaming tones, so people are *not* willing to answer or there is *no* learning for you or for them.

Bad questions do not improve the relationship with the other person, but rather worsen it and do not lead to the other person's awareness or growth. Bad questions make you think, "Why are you asking me that?" or "It's none of your business!"

Let me highlight three typical kinds of bad questions.

First, they lack consideration for the relationship with the other person. The question in the clothing store I mentioned earlier would be an example of this. Or questions like, "Do you have any debt?" or "How big is your current house?" might be acceptable in a situation like buying a new property at a real estate agency, but in most cases, the other person would feel uncomfortable.

Second, prying into the other person's private life without reason tends to lead to bad questions. Needless to say, it's necessary to exercise caution when asking about marriage, love, having children, or family relationships with someone you haven't established a good relationship with.

Third, questions that impose the questioner's values or assumptions on the other person, cornering or intimidating the other person, also tend to be bad questions.

Bad questions may unintentionally convey a negative message, even if you didn't intend to. For example, let's say a male employee asks a female colleague, "Don't you have any plans to get married?" If taken literally, he's just asking whether she plans to get married. To the male employee, this might be an extension of a conversation with a close friend, or he might be interested in her and wanted to know if she is "taken"! However, the question, "Don't you have any plans to get married?" could convey a message, a value imposition suggesting to the female colleague: "You may never get married, if you wait too long, and that's bad."

You might not have intended it that way, but remember, the message that was received by the other person is the message that was sent.

In other words, even if you had no intention of making the other person uncomfortable, if the other person received it that way, it's because you communicated it that way. Most bad questions are not made with ill intentions. That's why caution is necessary.

Additionally, "Don't you have any plans to get married?" uses a negative form ("don't you?"). Simply changing it to the positive form, "Do you . . . ?" might reduce the negative impression. We might often find ourselves asking, "Haven't you done your homework?" to a child, but "Is your homework done?" seems like an easier question to answer, doesn't it?

When asking questions, be mindful of whether you are unintentionally negating the other person. Choose your words carefully.

Heavy questions

"Why do you think you keep making this same mistake?"

That's heavy. That question hurts!

People are NOT willing to answer heavy questions asked by someone who hasn't established themselves as trustworthy.

But there is an opportunity for some deep learnings for you and for them.

Heavy questions are those that the other person may not want to answer, but they lead to realizations and actions. These questions touch on topics the other person may not want to think about, bring to consciousness, or usually avoid. And that's why they have a high potential to lead to realizations and actions. When used effectively, they can have a significant impact.

However, since these questions intrude into areas the other person may not want to touch, consideration and care are necessary.

When consciously using heavy questions, it's important to have established a good relationship with the other person and ask them at the right timing. It's also better to avoid repeatedly asking only heavy questions. Because these questions are heavy for the other person, it's necessary to give them time to think carefully. Mixing with some light questions might also encourage the other person to think about the answers to heavy questions.

Heavy questions could be similar to bad questions, you may say. But they have a fundamental difference.

In heavy questions, the purpose is shared. To prevent the other person from thinking, "Why is this person asking such a thing?", they need to recognize that the reason this person is asking such a tough question is for the sake of achieving their goals. To ask heavy questions, building a relationship and trust with the other person is essential, but without a shared purpose, they turn into bad questions.

Through my experience of asking heavy questions while presentation coaching numerous times, I realized that heavy questions have a significant effect of redirecting the other person's perspective toward themselves.

For example, I once asked the CEO of a mid-sized global accounting firm a heavy question: "Compared to outstanding CEOs around the world, where do you think you stand in terms of your abilities as a CEO?"

This CEO was in the process of creating a presentation to convey the purpose and effects of their company's initiative toward globalization. But some employees couldn't understand why the CEO had chosen to conduct the initiative in a certain way. When he heard this question, the CEO hesitated for a moment and admitted that he hadn't really thought about it.

We engaged in a series of questions and answers for a while, including these questions (these are considered GOOD questions. We will delve deeper soon):

"What are the differences between a global company like the Big Four and a mid-sized global company?"

"How much time are you dedicating to nurturing the next generation of leaders?"

"What do you think employees expect the most from a CEO?"

As we continued our conversations, the CEO realized that he had been blaming the employees for the company's struggle to advance in globalization, thinking they lacked effort. However, the question "How about yourself as a CEO of a global company?" prompted him to think from a self-reflective perspective.

Initially, the CEO had been thinking that globalization was not progressing because employees were not putting in enough effort. However, with the question about his role as a CEO of the company, that question became a catalyst for him to think from a different perspective. It became the "me-matter" from the "they-matter."

GOOD questions

Unlike the previous three types of questions, GOOD questions urge the other person to dig deeper into themselves to find answers within, and provide information *you* are looking for.

Examples of GOOD questions include:

- "What are three actions you will take next month to improve the situation?"
- "What expertise can you provide to help us achieve our sales goal?"
- "What are three actions you will take next month to improve the situation?"

- "Why do you think this became an issue?"
- "Who would be the right person to delegate this task to?"
- "Where does the potential bottleneck lie in this scenario?"
- "When are you going to complete this task?"
- "How are you going to motivate your team?"

GOOD questions bring out not just hidden information, but quality information. They provide great insight for you, and for them. And that's the key for effective communication to close the gap.

As I shared with you my experience with my coach, GOOD questions have power to Deepen, Widen, and Forward your thinking.

Here are some general rules of thumb to help you create GOOD questions:

- Adapt light questions by improving the awareness level
- Adapt heavy questions by improving the willingness to answer questions
- Think of questions in the vicinity of what's always in mind but has not been asked from that angle.

If you ask questions that the other person is always thinking about, or have been asked before, you won't gain much insight.

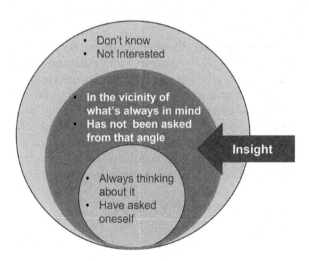

Explanation of GOOD questions

If you ask questions that are far from what they know or what they are interested in, they won't even know how to answer, or their answers will be quite shallow.

You need to find the blind spot in between the two to uncover insights.

What I want to emphasize is that, just like other three questions, there is no universally GOOD question. It's important to carefully consider the content based on the individual and customize what resonates the most with each one of them. Some GOOD questions may prompt significant insights in some individuals while not resonating with others at all. When asking questions, it's crucial to tailor them to each individual. It is the same approach as the "Culture of One."

Open-ended questions and closed-ended questions

GOOD questions often pertain to the future rather than the past and tend to be more open-ended rather than closed-ended.

Closed-ended questions limit responses to "Yes" or "No," such as

"Did you do your homework?"
"Did you contact the client?"

Closed-ended questions provide definite answers, so they are suited for situations when you need to clarify something, or when you want to confirm someone's intent.

In a power distance high culture, instructions and orders are often given from the top-down. So the higher the position, the higher tendency there is to use closed-ended questions to confirm whether the instructions have been followed through.

One of the benefits of using closed-ended questions is that they give less psychological burden to have to come up with lengthy answers on the spot, as they usually have only two options to choose from: yes or no.

However, a significant drawback of closed-ended questions is that the conversation may not expand beyond the limited answers of yes or no. Behind these one-word answers, you don't get to know what thoughts or motivations that led to those answers, why the actions were taken, or what the reasons or motives were. Additionally, if you repeat closed-ended questions, you may unintentionally convey suspicion to the other person.

For instance, when a mother asks a child,

"Did you do your homework?"

The child may perceive it not just as a confirmation of whether they did it or not, but also as the mother's suspicion that they haven't done their homework – again! Consequently, the child may become resentful and resistant. Yes, I'm guilty of that, too, with my daughter.

This applies in a work setting, as well. If a superior repeatedly uses closed-ended questions with subordinates, it can lead to a lack of trust.

On the other hand, open-ended questions allow for more freedom in responding compared to closed-ended questions.

Open-ended questions use the 5W1H (Who, What, When, Where, Why, and How) to explore the feelings and thoughts. Questions using "When," "Where," and Who" help clarify the other person's thoughts. Questions using "Why" and "How" encourage deeper thinking about the purpose of actions, the potential ramifications of those actions, and imagining the joy or benefits as a result of those actions.

Additionally, open-ended questions offer more flexibility in how the person answers, allow them to come up with answers and solutions themselves, and encourage spontaneous responses. Due to these characteristics, open-ended questions are often utilized in crafting GOOD questions.

If you tend to use more closed-ended questions, think about how you might be able to turn closed-ended questions into open-ended questions.

For example, the closed-ended question "Did you do your homework?" can be transformed into an open-ended question:

"What kind of homework do you have?"

Tips for High Context culture

You might recall from Chapter 1 that a High Context culture relies on surroundings and environment. It's not necessary – and can even be inappropriate – to spell everything out too explicitly. So listeners will be accustomed to reading between the lines – the "context" hiding under the surface. A general rule of thumb is that you want to use more open-ended questions to craft GOOD questions. When you are working with people from High Context cultures, open-ended questions encourage them to speak up. However, they may be stunned if an open-ended question is *too* open. For example,

"What did you think of our meeting?"

"How do you feel about their decision?"

Remember, High Context people tend to need permission to speak up, as they value maintaining harmony in the group. They don't want to disturb the harmony by selfishly offering their honest individualistic thoughts.

Here are three tips when crafting GOOD questions for High Context people:

1. Frame a question to prepare their mind

High Context people "read the atmosphere" and try to understand the context before answering questions. Frame a question so that they understand the purpose of your questions.
For example:

"I'd like to improve how to better facilitate the meeting next time. What did you think of our meeting?"
"I saw that you seemed uncomfortable when the decision was made. How do you feel about their decision?"

2. Be open but specific

While allowing them to answer openly, be specific with your question so that you can receive insightful answers.
For example, instead of asking "What did you think of our meeting?", you can adapt by asking "What did you like about the flow of today's meeting?" or "What did you think about everyone's participation level?"
This way, you are not giving your High Context respondent a huge room for interpretation of the intent of the question, but pinpointing the exact topic area you need an answer for.

3. Use closed-ended questions in between to confirm your understanding, their intention, and build a common ground

High Context people tend to communicate more indirectly and have room for interpretation. In order to avoid misinterpretation, use closed-ended questions in between to confirm their intention and to confirm that you are understanding them correctly.
For example: "What I took away from you is that you felt the meeting facilitator could have used more detailed agenda to facilitate the discussion more meaningfully. Am I understanding you correctly?"

Tips for asking good questions

As mentioned earlier, whether a question is considered a GOOD question depends on the context and the person being asked, so there's no "universally GOOD" questions. However, I can share with some strategies for asking GOOD questions that can be helpful in various situations.

1. Actively listen

First and foremost, a crucial attitude for asking good questions is to listen to the other person. In the previous chapter, we learned the three-step process of active listening: 1) show that you are listening, 2) show that you are understanding, and 3) ask GOOD questions. Showing a genuine interest and sincerely listening to the other person's words opens up the other person's heart. Active listening is more than a passive act of receiving a one-way message. It involves not only carefully listening to the other person's words but also seriously engaging with the emotions and the true intentions behind the words. It involves giving feedback to the other person, deepening their understanding, and enhancing their insights.

In addition to listening to the words spoken, it's important to pay attention to nonverbal cues. It becomes even more important when communicating with High Context people. The tone of voice, volume, speed of speech, body language, attire, posture, and facial expressions often convey more about one's feelings than words alone. By closely observing these cues, you can gather a lot of information about the other person's current state, making High Context communication an essential aspect of active listening. It's important to listen not only to what the person says but also to the emotions and the feelings conveyed through their words.

2. Adapt questions to the flow of the conversation

One of the fundamental aspects of asking GOOD questions is to adapt questions based on the flow of the conversation. While individualized preparation is essential, the key is to think on the spot and tailor questions to the ongoing conversation. Although I've emphasized the importance of individualized questions, it's a common mistake for beginners to simply recite prepared questions.

For instance, in job interviews, some students tend to deliver their self-introductions without considering the atmosphere and flow of the conversation. Pre-prepared words often don't capture the other person's attention. The same can be said about presentations. Many speakers recite the prepared script word by word. However, the audience is smart enough to tell when someone is simply reciting memorized words. Presentation is a two-way street. You deliver your message, the audience bounces back some sort of responses, mostly nonverbal but sometimes verbal, like "oooh!" "aaah!" If you completely ignore them and keep reciting words, you will lose your audience.

Similarly, sports broadcasts – for instance, football – might have a rookie TV announcer who's just reading out pre-prepared questions during post-game interviews. It's a shame because there might be interesting insights if they delve deeper into the responses by further questioning. If you pre-prepare all your questions, you're missing an opportunity to truly connect with the person right in front of you. By exploring the words more deeply, you could uncover intriguing aspects of that person.

Don't be mistaken, though. I am not saying that preparation is not important. It is! While it's important to be prepared and create a list of questions beforehand, during the actual session, it's crucial to be flexible and let the flow guide your questioning. You may have prepared 20 questions ahead of time but end up using just the first kick-start question. Do feel encouraged to branch off from one answer you received with more spontaneous questions.

3. Ask questions and avoid giving advice

While actively listening, it's important to refrain from giving advice. I know it's tempting. When I conduct a corporate workshop on active listening, most participants say during the debrief that the most challenging part of the active listening exercises was staying neutral and asking questions without giving advice. It is difficult for leaders to not jump into advice mode when they hear some-one's answer, particularly when they hear the person is struggling or needs help.

However, if you immediately come up with ideas for someone rather than staying neutral, the benefit is short lived. Your ideas may help someone for the time being, but they may not work in the future (after all, you may not be in possession of all the facts). Moreover, if you hand someone advice and signal that the other person should fol-low it, the other person won't be motivated to think proactively, and they'll be more likely to disengage. Ideas they come up on their own will have much more power than ideas given to them.

The same can be said when you are talking to your child. As a parent, we get the urge to give our children our expert advice. But we want our children to learn to become independent, form their own opin-ions, and solve challenging issues creatively on their own, right? They need to struggle – and sometimes fail – to learn a valuable lesson. Hard, I know. But we need to be patient, refrain from immediately providing advice or answers, and allow them to explore.

4. You-Focused questions

To ask good questions, having a "You-Focused" attitude is essential.

For example, if you want to ask questions that stimulate insights into how to achieve work goals, instead of asking about the industry environment or trends, it's more effective to gain insights by asking:

"What do you personally think about the current situation?"
"What do you believe should be done?"
"What does sustainability mean to you?"

Especially for those who tend to blame their environment for their work not going well, or use lack of support from subordinates or superiors as an excuse, asking a "You-Focused" question will wake them up and shift their focus from "they-matter" to "me-matter."

5. "I-Focused" feedback

The "You-Focused" approach is key in most effective communication. However, there are some occasions when an "I-Focused" approach becomes more effective – giving feedback.

In most cases, feedback comes in two parts – objective facts and subjective facts.

If I want to provide feedback on someone's presentation, objective facts may include the person's delivery habits, such as their tendency to use filler words, hand gestures, or poor eye contact. I would describe these facts as they are.

For example,

"In your presentation earlier, I heard 20 filler words. I also saw this hand gesture every time you said 'so.'"

Here again, no advice is given; just the facts are conveyed.

The other part is subjective facts. Unlike the objective facts mentioned earlier, this part has the potential of the other person taking it personally. When you use the "I-Focused" message, such as "I felt this way" or "I got this impression," you can ease the other person's emotions.

For example:

"I felt rushed when you were hopping through slides."
"I got the impression that you need more research to back up your data."

The important thing here is to avoid putting blame on the person. The subject is always "I," so that it's clear that it's your personal point of view. The person being told might feel unpleasant, but they can easily accept it as a fact that "this person felt this way."

However, if you convey it in a way that blames the person, saying, "You seem lackadaisical," the person will likely feel accused.

"I-Focused" messages are particularly effective not only in communication at work but also in situations like scolding children. Try them out and see how they react. It works every time with my preteen daughter.

How to craft GOOD questions

So far, we've learned how to turn a question you already want to ask into a GOOD question. Now, let's delve even further and discuss how to create GOOD questions from scratch – GOOD questions to Deepen, Widen, and Forward.

Have you ever told yourself, "Today, I'm going to create questions!"

Probably not. Not consciously.

However, we all unconsciously ask ourselves questions every day, if not every second.

"I have a meeting with a client at their office tomorrow at 10 a.m. What time do I need to leave home? What's the nearest station? Which subway lines do I take? Should I drive there? Where is the nearest parking garage then? What documents do I need to take to the meeting?"

Everyone goes through daily life asking themselves questions.

But these are not necessarily GOOD questions.

To experience where and how to find GOOD questions, let's do a quick exercise first.

Question: What questions do you ask yourself every day to enhance your quality of life? Take ten minutes and aim to come up with 20 questions. Don't worry about coming up with GOOD questions. Any questions are fine for the purpose of this exercise.

(Pause, take ten minutes, and write down your questions.)

Welcome back.

Some of you may easily come up with many questions, while some of you may struggle to think of more than five. That's totally fine.

Now, take a look at the list of questions you wrote down.

What kind of tendencies did you notice in the questions? Do you notice that similar questions keep coming up? Any common thread?

Many of your questions may be about your children, or about time management, or about finding hobbies.

Our values, desired goals, frequently used words, and perspectives are all different. These differences show up in your questions. Taking notice of this is the fundamental strategy for crafting GOOD questions.

Questions tend to become internalized without us noticing, and the same questions tend to be repeated unconsciously in our minds.

This means that if you want to ask GOOD questions – or in other words, if you want to give insights to the person you're questioning – you need to ask questions with new angles for that person – questions they have never asked themselves before.

Refer back to Figure on page 157. If the question being asked is the question you've asked yourself many times before, no new insights will arise. However, this doesn't mean asking questions completely unrelated to the person's interests and concerns. If the question is too far away from their interests, you also can't draw insights.

Insights, in fact, are never far from what the person is already thinking. The big insights for a person are also an extension of the knowledge and thoughts they have had up to that point. The effective way to create good questions is to find the gap close to the questions internalized within the person but are overlooked like blind spots.

Now, let's discuss how to strategically find *GOOD* questions. Again, we can use the 3-Step Process, The 3As.

First: Acknowledge

First, take notice of 3Vs while listening to the other person:

- Vision
- Values
- Vocabulary

Vision tells you what the person is aiming for, what they truly want, and what they sincerely want to achieve. Values are the fundamental beliefs the person feels important in life. Vocabulary is the words the person frequently uses in daily conversations.

When you actively listen to the other person, jot down keywords and acknowledge what Vision, Values, and Vocabulary stand out.

Since Vision and Values are both described with words, you may sometimes wonder which ones are Vision and Values, and which words should be categorized into Vocabulary. A general rule of thumb is that if a certain word is repeated a few times, categorize it as Vocabulary. There can be some duplicates between Vision/Values and Vocabulary. Don't spend too much time wondering how to categorize them, but rather, focus on jotting down important keywords. If you couldn't categorize them into 3Vs precisely, that's OK.

Second: Analyze

Next, analyze the Vision, Values, and Vocabulary you acknowledged.

When discussing Vision and Values, pay attention to the tone and expression the person uses – whether they sound anxious, passionate, or seem frustrated. Also pay attention to whether the person tends to use positive or negative words, or if certain words come up repeatedly. As explained before, it is crucial while active listening to analyze non-verbals while delving into the person's words, lifting them up, and uncovering what's hiding in the "iceberg."

Third: Adapt

Once you have collected enough keywords and done the analysis, it's time to adapt.

Combine 5W1H with the keywords – 3Vs – you jotted down. Here is an example.

Let's say, you jotted down the following keywords and roughly categorized them into 3Vs.

Vision

- I want to grow our revenue to over $5 million
- I want to improve employees' motivation
- I want my company to become No. 1 in the market
- I want my company to win the "best company to work for" award

Values

- Creativity facilitates innovation
- Open communication motivates employees
- Leaders should be facilitators
- I want to serve my employees
- Put others before me

Vocabulary

- No. 1
- Best
- Satisfaction: employee satisfaction, customer satisfaction, stakeholder satisfaction
- Our culture
- Leadership
- Serve
- Communication

Combining the 3Vs with 5W1H

Now, let's combine these 3Vs with 5W1H (Why, When, Where, What, Who, How) to strategically craft GOOD questions to Deepen, Widen, and Forward the thinking.

Deepening questions allow you to go deeper into the part of the iceberg you haven't or avoided tapped into.

Widening questions allow you to think outside the box and from different perspectives.

Forward questions allow you to determine which option you are going to take and how you can move forward with it.

See what you think

Think about the following as a guideline to craft "Deepening questions," "Widening questions," and "Forwarding questions."

Deepening questions

Deepening questions involve diving below the surface of the "iceberg," doubting the "common sense" or "assumptions," and uncovering the root causes of an issue. These questions force individuals to think critically, reflect on the issue at hand, and gain a more comprehensive understanding of the problem.

Here are some tips to craft deepening questions:

- **Challenge common sense and assumptions**. Begin by questioning the assumptions underpinning the problem. Ask, "What if this isn't true?" or "Why do we believe this is the core issue?" By doing so, you can challenge preconceived notions and open the door to fresh perspectives.
- **Identify root causes**. Probe further to discover the root causes of the problem. Ask "Why?" repeatedly, until you reach the most critical causes. This process helps peel away layers of symptoms to reveal the underlying issues.
- **Explore the consequences**. Examine the potential consequences of various solutions. Ask, "What are the implications of each option?" This helps in foreseeing unintended consequences and making more informed decisions.
- **Consider Different Perspectives.** Encourage diverse viewpoints by asking questions like, "How do others perceive this problem?" or "What might someone from a different background think about this?"; this can lead to innovative solutions by considering a wider range of experiences and knowledge.

Widening questions

Widening questions expand one's thoughts beyond the initial scope, encouraging consideration of broader contexts, external factors, and inter-connected issues. By thinking beyond the immediate thoughts, you can identify new angles and potential solutions.

Here are some tips to craft Widening questions:

- **Contextualize the problem: explore the broader context in which the problem exists.** Ask, "What external factors might be influencing this issue?"; this can help you understand the problem's significance in a larger framework.
- **Identify related issues: consider how the current problem might be linked to other challenges.** Pose questions like, "What are similar issues in different areas?" or "How might solving this problem impact other aspects of our work?"; identifying these connections can lead to holistic solutions.
- **Leverage analogies: use analogies to draw parallels between unrelated problems.** Ask, "What other domains or industries have faced similar challenges?"; drawing inspiration from diverse sources can yield creative solutions.
- **Forecast future trends: anticipate how the problem might evolve in the future.** Ask questions like, "What are the emerging trends in this area?" and "How might this problem change over time?"; this forward-thinking approach can help develop sustainable solutions beyond the current situation you are in.

Forwarding questions

Forwarding questions are instrumental in guiding the discussions toward actionable solutions. These questions encourage participants to transition from analysis to action, ultimately leading to the implementation of effective solutions. Here's how you can use Forwarding questions effectively:

- **Set clear objectives: begin by asking, "What do we want to achieve?".** Clearly defining objectives provides a sense of direction and purpose for the problem-solving process.
- **Brainstorm solutions: encourage ideation by asking, "What are some possible solutions?".** Emphasize quantity over quality in the initial brainstorming phase to ensure a wide range of ideas.
- **Evaluate and prioritize: ask, "Which solutions are most feasible, effective, and aligned with our objectives?".** Use criteria like cost, impact, and feasibility to prioritize ideas.

- Develop an action plan: move the discussion toward implementation by asking, "How can we execute these solutions?". Develop a detailed action plan with clear responsibilities and timelines.

With these tips in mind, go back to your exercise and go over the 3Vs again.

Pause as long as you need, and think about what *GOOD* questions you can come up with. Categorize them into "Deepening questions," "Widening questions," and "Forwarding questions."

Welcome back.

Following are some examples.

Deepening questions

- Why is *$5 million* the benchmark figure for your revenue growth? (Why + Vision)
- What do you want to achieve after winning the *"best company to work for" award*? (What + Vision)
- How would your *leadership* be viewed when you *put others before you*? (How + Values + Vocabulary)
- Who are the influential employees to *improve your culture*? (Who + Vocabulary)
- When do you feel that *open communication* is lacking to *motivate employees*? (When + Values + Vocabulary)
- Why is *becoming No. 1 in the market* your priority now? (Why + Vision + Vocabulary)

Widening questions

- What are some ways to improve *creativity to facilitate innovation*? (What + Values)
- If you have no limitation in resources, what would you do to achieve *No. 1 in the market*? (What + Vision + Vocabulary)
- What other awards might benefit in improving your brand awareness, other than the "best company to work for award"? (What + Vision)
- How does your *revenue growth over $5 million* affect your cost structure? (How + Vision)
- When do you think facilitative leadership may not work? (When + Values)

Forwarding questions

- Who is going to analyze the market opportunity to *grow your revenue to over $5 million*? (Who + Vision)

- When does the *growth revenue* opportunity analysis need to be finalized? (When + Vision)
- What's next after becoming *No. 1* in the industry? (What + Vocabulary)

I'm sure that you came up with a lot more variety of GOOD questions.

Now that you practiced strategically crafting GOOD questions with specific intentions, let's look at how you can use different questions to navigate the conversation to problem-solve or to bring conflict to consensus.

GOOD questions to problem-solve

In global teams, diversity of perspectives and cultural differences can lead to challenges and conflicts. The GOOD questioning technique is an effective approach in problem-solving in global teams.

GOOD questioning technique allows them to deepen and widen their thoughts, and move them forward with specific actions. If your global team is aiming to clarify Goals, explore Options, seek Opinions, and reach Decisions ("G-O-O-D"!), try maximizing the power of GOOD questions. Make sure you use Deepening questions, Widening questions, and Forwarding questions in open-ended style as well as closed-ended style strategically.

The true power of the combination of these GOOD questions is realized when they are seamlessly integrated into the problem-solving process. A well-structured problem-solving process might progress through these phases. This process can be used in one-on-one communications as well as facilitated team discussions, as follows.

1. Understand the situation

Ask light questions to break the ice, build rapport, and gain trust. Effectively use open and closed-ended questions interchangeably to set the tone, so that the other person is comfortable to open up, feel heard and understood, and ready to go deeper.

2. Extract issues/problems

Intentionally use more open-ended questions to identify the issue or problem. You may still use some closed-ended questions to confirm what has been said and to build a common understanding for all participants.

This is where GOOD questions would play crucial roles. If high-quality GOOD questions are not posed, discussions could stay superficial, and you may not reach the root causes of the issues. If you are solving a wrong problem, the solution becomes obsolete. Utilize Deepening questions and Widening questions in this phase.

3. Brainstorm solutions

In the brainstorming phase, you do not evaluate options yet. Utilize Widening questions to go outside the box, help participants put on others' shoes, and expand their horizons.

4. Evaluate options

To evaluate options, challenge participants by further deepening their thoughts. What are the criteria to make decisions? Why is this option the best option? You may need to ask some heavy questions to challenge their thoughts here, as this is the final chance before making the decision. If the discussions go around and around, you may need Forwarding questions to move participants to the next phase.

5. Make decision

Use Forwarding questions to lead participants toward the action plans. Use open-ended questions, as well as closed-ended questions, to confirm who takes what action, when.

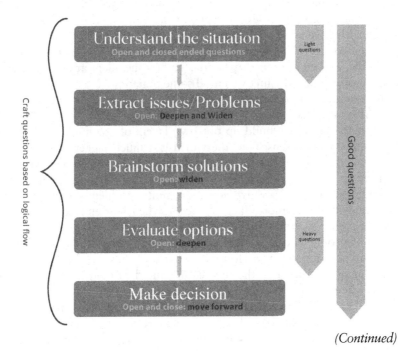

(Continued)

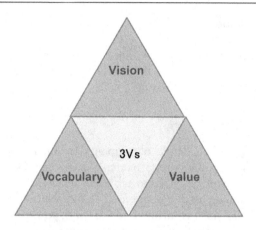

Explanation of problem-solving

GOOD questions you need to be asking yourself to become a true global leader

The power of GOOD questions go beyond one-on-one communications or global team communications. A global leader who would inspire the people around them – regardless of culture, values, or generations – is a person who is attractive as a human being.

When you learn to ask yourself GOOD questions, you will enrich your work life, as well as your private life. To become adept at asking GOOD questions in your daily life, you need some practice.

I encourage you to meet with and talk to people from different cultures and different fields.

Over the years, we build up our own layers of assumptions, and they form our common sense. But the world is a much bigger place. Talking to people from different cultures and different fields can provide you with entirely new perspectives. While it might seem that talking to people closer to your background can give you more hints, problem-solving, insights, and innovation are more likely to occur when you engage with people who are different from you. When a young newcomer joins a team composed of people who have worked together for years, it may temporarily revert to a storming stage. However, what was considered common sense before might not be so for the new recruit, and their unique perspective can breathe new life into the team.

Also, keep asking yourself "So What?" "Why So?" five times.

Among many valuable techniques I learned at McKinsey, one that stands out to me is "So What?" "Why So?". This approach, reminiscent of the

Toyota Production System, "Kaizen," involves asking "So What?" "Why So?" five times to find the points that need improvement. This process is crucial, because once you identify a problem, you cannot determine its true cause until you have eliminated all misunderstandings.

For example, if one production line suddenly stops when other lines only stop once a month, the initial question is: "Why did that particular production line stop?" However, you won't reach the root cause with this question alone. The cause could be multiple issues, such as a poorly designed shift schedule or changes in the car model that make it less efficient. By repeatedly asking "So What? Why So?", you can start to see the underlying factors.

You can ask this question to your own self-development – "self-Kaizen" – as well.

To excel on the global stage, you need to acquire a broad sense of cultural differences and commonalities between your home culture and others. While learning the 3As as discussed in this book is essential, there is one question I'd like you to keep asking yourself:

"What uniqueness do I possess?"

Your uniqueness could be your experience, perspective, specific skillset, upbringing, or hobby you are passionate about. This uniqueness that only you possess is what makes you stand out as a global leader.

Your uniqueness is your gift to the world.

Instead of just learning from the world, remember that you have something unique to offer to the world. As globalization advances, it's crucial to acknowledge your uniqueness, analyze it, and adapt it to serve the world in your own unique way. The world will increasingly demand individuals who can embrace and utilize their unique qualities.

Note

1 *Yes, Prime Minister*, episode 6, "A Victory for Democracy," directed by Sydney Lotterby, written by Antony Jay and Jonathan Lynn, featuring Paul Eddington, Derek Fowlds, and Nigel Hawthorne, aired February 13, 1986, on BBC, 13:05–13:54, https://www.dailymotion.com/video/x5t4iz6.

Putting it all together, and the Bonus A

Remember Bill? The top salesperson at a large American apparel wholesale company who went to Japan and failed big?

After that incident, Bill worked with me and learned the 3As and how to apply them to present to the global audience persuasively, to manage and motivate his team effectively, and to connect one-on-one at the personal level authentically. He was able to learn from his mistake, apply the 3As and become a much more effective leader and communicator.

This didn't happen overnight. At first, Bill was headstrong, because he prided himself in how he had achieved his success as a top salesperson in his company. Much like a dancer learning a new routine, Bill needed to commit to improving – and practicing the steps! What really made him grow as a global leader beyond his company, beyond his country, and beyond his comfort zone, was when he embraced what I call the Bonus A, and shifted his attitude to "Yes, AND."

A few years later, Bill's company acquired a global company. He became the leader of one of the merged divisions. He now shares his knowledge with his team members so they – as a team – can be effective, productive, dynamic, persuasive . . . and thus convey their all-important One BIG Message internally, externally, locally, and globally.

You, too, can become an effective global leader and communicator.

Throughout these pages, you've embarked on a transformative journey, navigating the 3-Step Process that has empowered you to present your ideas effectively and persuasively, not only locally but also globally. You've learned the power of clarity, connection, and impact. You've honed your skills in uncovering a unique One BIG Message, crafting compelling stories, engaging your audience, facilitating your team and navigating them through different stages, and asking powerful questions to better understand and to be understood.

But beyond the strategies and techniques, you've discovered the true essence of your One BIG Message. Although One BIG Message is the most important message in your presentation and other communications, it also represents your core beliefs, your values, your brand. It's not just about persuading others or gaining recognition; it's about sharing a part of yourself that can inspire change, spark innovation, and make the world a better place. And what ties everything together is the Bonus A: the "Yes, AND" attitude.

The "Yes, AND" attitude can play a significant role in cross-cultural situations, and uncovering and presenting your One BIG Message® effectively and persuasively.

- Cultural sensitivity: Cross-cultural communication often requires a heightened level of cultural sensitivity. The "Yes, AND" attitude encourages you to Acknowledge and respect cultural differences. It's about saying "Yes" to the cultural nuances and perspectives of others, "And" to find common ground and mutual understanding.
- Openness to diversity: In a cross-cultural context, diversity is a given. The "Yes, AND" attitude promotes embracing this diversity as a source of strength. It encourages you to appreciate the richness of different cultural backgrounds and perspectives, allowing your message to resonate with a broader range of people.
- Adaptability: as we learned in the 3As, cross-cultural interactions often require adaptability and flexibility. The "Yes, AND" attitude encourages you to Adapt your communication style and message to the cultural norms and expectations of your audience. It's about being open to new ways of presenting your ideas that align with the cultural context.
- Empathy and connection: Building strong connections in cross-cultural communication is essential. The "Yes, AND" attitude emphasizes empathy and active listening. By saying "Yes" to the experiences and emotions of others and "*and*" to showing understanding and support, you can bridge cultural gaps and create deeper connections.
- Conflict resolution: Cross-cultural interactions may sometimes lead to misunderstandings or conflicts. The "Yes, AND" attitude can be a valuable tool for conflict resolution. It encourages finding common ground and working collaboratively to resolve issues rather than escalating conflicts.
- Collaboration and connection: In presenting your ideas, connecting with your audience is essential. The "Yes, AND" attitude encourages collaboration and building connections with others. When you're open to the input and feedback of your audience, you create a sense of engagement and collaboration. This not only makes your message more persuasive, but also helps you connect with your audience on a deeper level.
- Embracing creativity: The "Yes, AND" attitude is closely linked to creativity. It encourages a mindset whereby you build upon existing ideas

and generate new ones. When crafting your One BIG Message, being creative and thinking outside the box can help you find unique ways to present your ideas effectively and persuasively.

In a cross-cultural context, the "Yes, AND" attitude serves as a bridge for effective and persuasive communication. It allows you to navigate the complexities of diverse cultures with respect and openness, promoting mutual understanding and collaboration.

Additionally, incorporating the "Yes, AND" attitude into your journey of uncovering your One BIG Message means being open to new possibilities, embracing collaboration, and fostering a growth mindset. It can help you not only present your message more effectively but also create a dynamic and engaging experience for your audience.

By saying "Yes, AND" to the world and the people you interact with, you'll be better equipped to make a lasting and persuasive impact with your message.

At the beginning of this book, you wondered, "Is there something I can do to learn effective cross-cultural communication?".

By now, I hope you can answer that question with a resounding "Yes!"

And you are ready to embark on your cross-cultural journey to uncover your One BIG Message and present your ideas effectively and persuasively, globally and locally.

Endnote

Growing up in Japan, I learned to read between the lines.

When I immigrated to the United States, I quickly learned that what made me successful there wasn't going to take me where I wanted to go. But it took me over a decade to find out *how* I can get where I want to go.

This book gives you a huge shortcut.

However, just like you can't become a great dancer by reading about techniques in a book, you must apply your knowledge to actions. I encourage you to take it from a ballroom into a boardroom and beyond.

Your cross-cultural journey has just begun. And it's a lifelong journey. I'm still learning, too.

I would love to share my experience in a keynote speech at your next event.

I would love to train your leadership team to help them excel as global leaders.

I would love to hear your personal experience in private coaching sessions.

Feel free to reach out to me by visiting **www.natsuyolipschutz.us**.

Parting thoughts

As I conclude this book, I want to extend my heartfelt gratitude to the individuals and organizations that have been instrumental in bringing this project to fruition. The journey of writing and sharing "Uncover Your One BIG Message®" has been a remarkable one, and it wouldn't have been possible without the support, inspiration, and collaboration of some exceptional people.

First and foremost, I want to express my deepest appreciation to Ken Lizotte and Elena Petricone of Emerson. Ken, your unwavering belief in my vision and your constant encouragement have been my guiding light. Elena, your dedication to making my book a reality has been a true source of inspiration. I am profoundly grateful for both of your support during this journey. I would like to offer a special thanks to Pam Harper of Business Advancement Inc., who introduced me to Ken and Elena. Your role as a catalyst in bringing like-minded individuals together to share their knowledge and passion is truly commendable.

To Meredith Norwich, the senior editor at Routledge, and everyone in her team, thank you for believing in the potential of this book and for your commitment to helping authors share their ideas with the world. Your professionalism and expertise have made this journey a smooth and enriching one.

I would like to extend my gratitude to my fellow HEROIC (Heroic Public Speaking) friends. Back in 2019, I had a professional speakers training at HEROIC. Since then, I've been meeting with my accountability group on a weekly basis. Your enthusiasm for personal and professional development, as well as your genuine care to making a positive impact, has been a constant source of inspiration. This book is a testament to the power of individuals coming together to learn, grow, and inspire one another.

When this book was in development, I earned my Certified Speaking Professional (CSP®). The CSP® designation is conferred by The National Speakers Association (NSA), and it stands as the supreme benchmark for professional speaking skills with a proven track record and experience.

Fewer than 17% of NSA members worldwide hold this distinguished title. I am truly honored and humbled to become the first Japanese and one of a few Asians to receive this designation.

Finally, to my family – my husband Rob and daughter Leena. Day after day, between my speaking engagements, strategy consulting projects, cooking, and house chores, I kept writing at home, at office, and often at ice skating rink where Leena trains as a competitive figure skater. Sometimes I got stuck, and Leena would give me tough love to keep going. I am deeply appreciative of both of your love and encouragement. I hope this book serves as a reminder of the power of a shared journey toward self-discovery, and personal and professional growth.

I hope that the readers of this book – wherever you are in the world – find value in the ideas presented and are inspired to uncover and share your own One BIG Message. Remember that your voice and message have the power to influence, educate, and create positive change in the world.

Thank you to all who have been a part of this journey, and may your own journeys be filled with discovery, growth, and the joy of connecting in the world, one message at a time.

With heartfelt gratitude,

Natsuyo Nobumoto Lipschutz

Bibliography

Aristotle. Aristotle's *"Art of Rhetoric."* Translated by Robert C. Bartlett. 1st ed. Chicago: University of Chicago Press, 2019.

Brown, Brené. "Don't Be Afraid to Fall: Brené Brown Addresses the University of Texas at Austin's 2020 Graduates." The University of Texas at Austin. May 24, 2020. YouTube video, 21:07. https://youtu.be/wMV77x YdEa4?si=UCaFTMIy_ZfsyGzj.

The Culture Factor. "Country Comparison Tool," accessed February 27, 2024. https://www.hofstede-insights.com/country-comparison-tool. License for use granted by The Culture Factor Group – Hofstede Insights Oy.

Field, Syd. *Screenplay: The Foundations of Screenwriting.* Revised ed. New York: Delta, 2005.

Giberti, Mica. "Logic – Is It Logical?" In *Rhetoric in Everyday Life*, edited by Alessandra Von Burg. Montreal: PressBooks, 2021. https://librarypartnerspress.press books.pub/rhetoricineverydaylife/chapter/logic-is-it-logical-by-mica-giberti/.

Hall, Edward T. *Beyond Culture.* New York: Anchor Books, 1977.

Hofstede, Geert. *Culture's Consequences: Comparing Values, Behaviors, Institutions, and Organizations Across Nations.* 2nd ed. Thousand Oaks: Sage Publications, 2003.

Lewin, Kurt. "Frontiers in group dynamics: Concept, method and reality in social science; social equilibria and social change." *Human Relations* 1, no. 1 (June 1947): 5–41. https://doi.org/10.1177/001872674700100103.

Lotterby, Sydney, dir. *Yes, Prime Minister.* Season 1, episode 6, "A Victory for Democracy." Aired on February 13, 1986, on BBC. https://www.dailymotion.com/video/x5t4iz6.

Ma, Jack. "Jack Ma: I've Had Lots of Failures and Rejections." World Economic Forum. February 3, 2015. YouTube video, 44:32. https://youtu.be/1O3ghiyirvU ?si=bjobzF18fA4qbj0R.

Obama, Michelle. "Michelle Obama's DNC speech." PBS NewsHour. August 17, 2020. YouTube video, 18:31. https://www.youtube.com/watch?v=uKy3iiWjhVI.

SOPTV ED, and Harrison, Robert. "Iceberg Concept Images and PDF's." Infographic. PBS LearningMedia, accessed April 3, 2024. https://indiana.pbslearningmedia.org/resource/a353a4ba-cd56-4999-97dd-0e40e11a7211/iceberg-concept-of-culture-images-and-pdfs/.

Tuckman, Bruce W. "Developmental sequence in small groups." *Psychological Bulletin* 63, no. 6 (June 1965): 384–399. https://doi.org/10.1037/h0022100.

Watson, Emma. "Emma Watson at the HeforShe Campaign 2014." United Nations. September 22, 2014. YouTube video, 13:15. https://youtu.be/gkjW9PZBRfk?si= Z4gfp6wuA2RrgVFt.

Index

Note: Numbers in *italics* indicate a figure on the corresponding page